1971

THE AMERICAN
COLONIAL CHARTER

A Da Capo Press Reprint Series

THE ERA OF THE AMERICAN REVOLUTION

GENERAL EDITOR: LEONARD W. LEVY

Claremont Graduate School

The American Colonial Charter

*A Study of English Administration
in Relation
Thereto, Chiefly After 1688*

By Louise Phelps Kellogg

DA CAPO PRESS · NEW YORK · 1971

A Da Capo Press Reprint Edition

This Da Capo Press edition of *The American Colonial Charter* is an unabridged republication of the first edition published originally in 1904 as part of the *Annual Report of the American Historical Association for the Year 1903*, Volume I. The pagination of the first edition has been retained in square brackets to facilitate reference to citations based on that edition.

Library of Congress Catalog Card Number 71-75291
SBN 306-71292-X

Published by Da Capo Press, Inc.
A Subsidiary of Plenum Publishing Corporation
227 West 17th Street, New York, N.Y. 10011

Manufactured in the United States of America

THE AMERICAN COLONIAL CHARTER.

By Louise Phelps Kellogg, Ph. D.

CONTENTS.

INTRODUCTION.

In the study of the American Revolution, and the causes that led to the breaking away of so large a body of colonists from the mother country, attention has chiefly been centered since the heat of the controversy has died away upon the economic aspects of the problem. To the navigation laws and the mercantile system has been traced the underlying irritation that blazed forth into the American revolt. Some

[187]1

recent studies, however, have tended to show that the damage
inflicted upon the American colonies by the policy of trade
was not so great as has been assumed, and that the causes
for dissatisfaction thereat are scarcely adequate to account
for so great a breach. Attention has, therefore, reverted
to the governmental and administrative system to discover
if the growing democracy of the American colonies found
itself hampered and out of relation to the government under
which it was developing. The results of these studies have
been fruitful in showing, at least, that the colonial dissatisfaction and alienation was not a sudden matter consequent
upon the Stamp Act and the increased activity of the English
administrators following the French and Indian war; but that
its roots lie deeper, and can be traced for the life of at least
three generations; and that the administrative system had
been felt during that entire period as an irritating factor at
enmity with the natural development of colonial life. This
study is a contribution to that line of investigation. It takes
up the class of colonies not under the direct administration of
the English officials—colonies removed from their immediate
supervision by the previous grant of charter rights and privileges—and attempts to show, in a somewhat detailed manner
and for a limited period, how the English administration
pressed upon these granted privileges, asserted the prerogative within their limits, and endeavored entirely to abrogate
them by acts of Parliament.[a]

The paper deals with a period in which the activity of the
Board of Trade and Plantations proved itself a real factor in
American colonial government. This period opens with the
creation of the Board of Trade and Plantations, and the navigation act of 1696 that accompanied it—an act imposing new
restrictions on governors, and providing for a colonial admiralty court. It closes practically with the reversion of the
Carolina governments to the Crown (1719). The method of
treatment is not chronological, but, instead, several lines of
investigation are separately pursued throughout the period,

[a] Since this monograph was written the able work of Prof. Herbert L. Osgood, The
American Colonies in the Seventeenth Century (New York, 1904), has appeared, showing
that the proprietary type was the more primitive and rudimentary form of colonial
organization, which was being superseded at the close of the seventeenth and beginning
of the eighteenth century by the more closely administered royal province. The importance of the transition period, with which this paper deals, is thus thrown into clearer
relief.

in order to render more clear the policy of the board, as evinced by its specific acts. After the introductory data furnished by the first chapter, chapter 2 deals with the action of the administration in regard to specific colonies, the attempt to take advantage of every situation, a flaw in the title, disorder in the colonies, an opportunity to purchase, in order to dispose of the charter privileges, and bring the colony in question under the direct control of the Crown. Chapter 3 takes up a different series of actions. It attempts to show that the English administrators took every opportunity to assert the royal prerogative within the limits of the colonies under proprietary or corporation government; that in the matter of the executive, they endeavored to secure control over the governors not appointed by the Crown; that they established courts within colonies, where the right of erecting judicial tribunals had been granted away, and drew over appeals from colonial courts in all the colonies, however administered; finally, that in the matter of legislation, the board of trade tried to establish supervision over the acts of all the legislatures and to assert the right of royal veto. The third line of policy was more direct, and relied upon the newly developed theory of Parliamentary omnipotency. The attempt was several times made to pass an act in Parliament vacating all colonial charters at once. These various bills are discussed in chapter 4—the causes for their introduction and the reasons for their failure set forth in some detail.

Incidentally, the paper attempts to give an idea of the divided responsibility and imperfect workings of the system of English colonial administration. Its methods were cumbrous; there was lack of a direct connection with the colonies, and complete or satisfactory knowledge of their conditions, needs, and desires. A ready ear was lent to complaints against them, and a spirit of general suspicion rather than of cordial cooperation was evinced. The organs of the home government charged with the control of colonial affairs grew less and less efficient. Vexatious delays and disappointments ensued for those who sought redress. The hindrances due to the physical separation, especially the time required to exchange communications, put the entire system out of relation to the needs of colonial life. The feelings of the colonists toward this system are also in a measure revealed. The

4[190]   AMERICAN HISTORICAL ASSOCIATION.

conditions of pioneer life in America had begun to transform
the character of the colonists and to free them from the
domination of English ideas. The vast stretch of new lands,
the economic opportunities, the influx of foreign elements had
begun by the close of the seventeenth century to produce a
democratic spirit in the colonies that asserted itself through
the colonial legislature in opposition to the royal agents, and
in resistance to English methods of administration. The
colonies which were sheltered behind charters showed the
most independent spirit. Those under proprietors felt less
restrained by their relation to subjects than if they had been
directly controlled by the Crown; so that with the progress
of the century the position of proprietor grew more difficult,
and his relation to the colonists more constantly strained. In
the corporation colonies an almost complete system of local
independence and self-government grew up, insomuch that
Connecticut and Rhode Island maintained their constitutions
unchanged after the Revolution, and lived under their charters
well into the nineteenth century. The resistance in these colonies, therefore, to interference with their chartered privileges
was sturdy, and their opposition to the policy of the Board of
Trade was firm. Moreover, the latter body was influenced
by the pronounced enemies of the corporations, and if the
English administrators regarded these colonies with especial
suspicion, the feeling of resentment and opposition toward the
board on the part of the colonists verged at times on open
hostility. Thus were the seeds sown that ripened into revolution. The English administrative system had proved not
only inadequate and ill-adjusted, but even instrumental in
alienating from the Crown of England its richest and most
valued possessions.

In the preparation of this monograph assistance in the form
of encouragement and suggestion has been liberally given.
Especial thanks are due to Mr. Hubert Hall, of His Majesty's
Public Record Office, London, whose kindness and courtesy
are indicative of his interest in American historical research.
Acknowledgment is also offered to Professors Frederick J.
Turner and Paul S. Reinsch of the University of Wisconsin,
to Professor Charles M. Andrews of Bryn Mawr College, and
to Professor Charles H. Hull, of Cornell University, for timely
criticism and interest.

MADISON, WIS., *March, 1904.*

Chapter I.

THE INCEPTION AND CONTROL OF ENGLISH COLONIES.

Indirect colonization by individuals and corporations—Charters as authorization—Charters before the Restoration—Royal colonies by forfeiture and conquest—Post-Restoration grants—Subinfeudation—Stuart forfeitures—Effect of Revolution of 1688—Privy Council—Board of Trade—Experiments in founding—Reestablishment—Personnel—Policy—Secretary of State—Admiralty—Commissioners of customs—Colonial agents.

The English Crown has never been a colonizing agency. Its vast colonial empire has been built up partly by private initiative, authorized or unauthorized, and partly by conquest. Of the colonies founded in the New World during the seventeenth century the larger ones were all authorized in some manner. The unauthorized colonies were small and insignificant, either offshoots from the larger or established upon lands previously granted to others. Such were the fishing colonies of Newfoundland and Maine, the trading colonies of New Hampshire and North Carolina, and the agricultural colonies with a religious basis—Plymouth, Rhode Island, Connecticut, and New Haven. Sooner or later all of these unauthorized colonies either lost their separate existence—as Plymouth and the settlements in Maine subjected to Massachusetts Bay, New Haven merged into Connecticut—or else were erected into authorized colonies, as New Hampshire, North Carolina, and Barbados granted to proprietors, Rhode Island and Connecticut given a charter of incorporation. If, therefore, we disregard as temporary the colonies that grew up unauthorized by the English Government—interesting though the type of compact government is which they developed, and persistent though its influence has been upon American local institutions [a]—we may say that English colonization in America was undertaken by two classes of agencies: one, familiar to the merchant class, the corporation for trade and settlement; the other, equally familiar to the landed gentry, the fief or proprietorship. In both cases the means of governmental authorization was a charter.

---

[a] See Turner, "Western State making in the Revolutionary era," in American Historical Review, 1895, pp. 266–268.

The first and most natural form of colonial enterprise was due to individual initiative, the desire of some needy noble or daring younger son to carve out for himself an estate on the virgin continent, where land was to be had for the asking. The first form of the colonizing charter, therefore, was a fief, but a fief of a special type, that known as a county palatine, suitable to outlying portions of the kingdom, where the exigencies of defense and protection needed a government almost sovereign, trammeled but little by the central power. Such were the counties palatine of Chester and Durham, and under a charter granting a fief of this type Cabot started forth on his discoveries. In 1598 the palatinate charter was revived for Sir Humphrey Gilbert, who had authority to settle and govern the lands he should discover,[a] and Raleigh's lost colony of Roanoke was a proprietorship in embryo.

As the fief was familiar to the landed proprietors, so was the trading company to the merchants.[b] The earliest company organized in England for the foreign trade grew up in the Low Countries, and had civil and criminal jurisdiction over its own servants. In 1564 it was incorporated under a charter as "The Fellowship of Merchants Adventurers," and its seat was removed to Hamburg. Closely following this model, the Eastland Company (1579) and the Levant or Turkey Company (1581) were incorporated. The East India Company (1600) was established not only for trade, but for "the discovery of lands, isles, territories, dominions, and seigniories unknown, and not before the late adventure by sea or navigation commonly frequented."[c]

The charters of both these colonizing agencies had certain marked characteristics that determined the course of institutional development in America. The term charter (carta) was originally applied to the piece of parchment upon which the instrument was written. In the later Roman Empire and

---

[a] See Prince Society Publications, Sir Humphrey Gylberte (Boston, 1903), pp. 95–102.

[b] An interesting link between the two classes of charters is that granted to the Earl of Southampton in 1610, establishing a fishing company, but with features of a fief. See "Attempts at Colonizing New England, Merchant Adventurers of Bristol," in Amer. Hist. Rev., July, 1899.

[c] Clause from the charter of the Muscovy Company. Hakluyt, Collection of Early Voyages (London, new ed., 1812), I, 267. The literature on chartered colonies is large. The following are suggestive works: Wallis, "Early colonial constitutions," in Royal Historical Society Transactions, new series, X, 1896; Bonnassieux, Les Grandes Compagnies de Commerce (Paris, 1890); Egerton, Short History of British Colonial Policy (London, 1897).

the Roman Church it gradually came to signify the deed or instrument itself. Introduced into England through ecclesiastical agencies, a charter, by its greater importance, although frequently used interchangeably with deed or patent, soon became differentiated, and was usually concerned with a grant of land, although Magna Charta and charters of pardons remind one that the chief significance of the term was the grant of privileges. Hobbes says, "Charters are donations of the sovereign, and not laws, but exemptions from law."[a]

In the charter of the palatinate fief, the source of government and authority was the proprietor, to whom were granted the jurisdictions, liberties, immunities, regalities, and franchises which were enjoyed by the Bishop of Durham, including the right to grant lands, appoint officers, erect tribunals, establish militia, control the church, incorporate towns, designate ports, and assess customs, in return for which he was to protect the colony, turn over one-fifth of all precious metals discovered, and yield allegiance to the Crown. The form of government, in other words, was to be monarchical, proceeding from the proprietor downward to the colony. The one check upon this almost unlimited authority of the proprietor was the legislative assembly, which he was to constitute "by and with the assent, advice, and approbation of the freemen of said province." Probably this was intended to act in some measure like a county court, and become the means of publication and promulgation of laws, and of assessing taxes; but under the pressure of American social democracy, it developed into an organ of popular expression and the seat of resistance to the proprietor's power. As the chief purpose of the proprietary charter was to found a landed estate, the statute of "quia emptores" was in every case suspended and the proprietor given the power of erecting manors, of selling and alienating lands. The proprietary, therefore, was a vast estate, and the relation between the colonists and the head of the province was complicated, because of this twofold relation as governor and governed, landlord and tenant.

The charters granted to corporations provided for two sorts of government, that of the company itself, with its courts, officers, and freemen; and that for the colony established

---

[a] Hobbes, Leviathan (ed. of 1839), p. 276.

within their jurisdiction.   With regard to the latter the powers of the corporations were even greater than those of proprietors, since each company had full authority to nominate officers for its colony, to ordain its laws, to pardon, govern, and rule all subjects who should adventure there, so that the laws ordained be not "contrarie to the Lawes of this our realm of England."

The charters issued to companies for purposes of trade differ from the proprietary charters issued to create an estate chiefly by the former's regulations for commerce, and by its internal regulations.   As far as the English administrators were concerned, the colonies founded by corporations were as far removed from their sphere of action as were those founded by proprietors; the difference between a single proprietor, or a company of proprietors, was not of consequence to the English official.   Indeed, several of the later proprietaries were governed by boards—for example, Carolina and the Bahamas.   The main feature was that the colony, while owing allegiance to the Crown, was removed from its direct jurisdiction by the immunities granted by the charter.[a]

CHARTERS BEFORE THE RESTORATION.

The period of the early Stuarts was one of frequent grants of charters both to corporations and proprietors.   For a liberal prince, such as each Stuart wished to seem, nothing was easier than to divide up unknown lands in this lavish fashion. If the enterprise succeeded it redounded to the glory and extension of the monarchy; if it failed, the prince was none the worse.   It was a convenient method of rewarding courtiers, paying obligations, and dispensing favors at little or no pecuniary cost.   Therefore, when the colonizing era once began, the entire continent of North America and the outlying islands were soon parceled out into fiefs for the noblemen of the court.

In 1623 Lord Baltimore received a grant of a portion of Newfoundland, where he attempted to found the colony of Avalon, as an asylum for Romanists; but the climate proving too bleak for their ardor, he was compensated by a grant of

---

[a] As an evidence of the attitude of the English administrative office the papers of certain colonies are classified in the Colonial office as "Proprieties," including both corporation and proprietary colonies.

Maryland (1632). Nova Scotia was granted to Sir William Alexander in 1621, and although the French claim to prior occupation was conceded by the Treaty of St. Germain in 1632, Alexander's rights were purchased by the French proprietors. In 1629 Sir Robert Heath, the king's attorney-general, obtained a charter for Carolana (the district south of Virginia); but, the colony failing, he disposed of his patent to the Earl of Arundel. Part of this was afterwards merged in Carolina; but Daniel Cox bought up the southern portion, for which he never obtained royal confirmation. Sir Ferdinando Gorges, chief mover in the Plymouth council, secured a royal charter for his share of the corporation's lands, which he erected into the proprietorship of Maine, and for it established a local government in 1640. That this did not prove to be another large American fief was doubtless due to Gorges's preoccupation with the political troubles in England. The rights of his heirs were purchased by Massachusetts in 1677. The long chain of islands off the Caribbean Sea, on which some small English settlements had been made, were patented to the Earl of Carlisle in 1627.[a] Although the French made good their prior claim to some of the islands, Carlisle instituted a proprietary government for Barbados, which existed until 1663. But two of these fiefs, Maryland and Barbados, developed into permanent colonial governments. For the purpose of colony founding, therefore, the proprietary charter proved less efficacious than the charter organizing a corporation.

In 1606 James I issued a charter which is unique in that it established two councils, not companies, one at London for Virginia, the other at Plymouth for the northern territory in America. Both councils, however, received incorporation by means of later and more adequate patents. That for the London Company was issued in 1609, creating the "Treasurer and Company of Adventurers and Planters of the City of London, for the first colony of Virginia," and giving them

---

[a] The vacillating policy of Charles I is epitomized in the history of this charter. "The Earl of Marlborough had a prior grant of Barbados. Carlisle compromised with him for an annuity of £300. Later the King granted to the Earl of Montgomery a patent for Trinidad, Tabago, Barbudos, and Fonseca." Carlisle protested, and the latter grant was revoked. The terms of Carlisle's charter are similar to those of Baltimore. Sainsbury, ed., Calendar State Papers, Colonial Series, America and West Indies (London, 1860-1902.) I, 85, 242.

rights of managing the affairs of the company, as well as
rights of government for the colony they had planted. In
1612 a third charter enlarged their boundaries by the grant
of all islands within 300 leagues of the coast. These were surrendered, however, three years later, upon the incorporation
of the Bermuda Company, which had purchased the London
Company's rights to the islands.

Under the second, or Plymouth council, a colony had been
attempted on the coast of Maine. After its failure the promoters of the enterprise sought and obtained, in 1620, a charter
from King James, making them a body corporate by the name
of the Council for New England, with full rights of government over the territory between the fortieth and forty-eighth
degree of north latitude. The policy of the council for New
England was to make two sorts of grants, one to small planters
with quit-rent titles, and one with powers of government to
those undertaking to plant a large colony. The Plymouth
colony secured a patent of the latter kind from the council
for New England, but it was never confirmed by the Crown.
The Massachusetts Bay Company, more fortunate, secured a
royal charter of incorporation in 1629. The council for New
England made a second attempt to plant a colony under Robert
Gorges in 1623, but its plans for colonies proved abortive and
it finally came into disfavor with Parliament. Thereupon several of the incorporators became dissatisfied and withdrew.
The company maintained a desultory existence until 1635,
when it voluntarily resigned its charter to the King. Still
another "Governor and Company" were incorporated the year
after that of Massachusetts Bay for the islands of Providence,
Henrietta, etc., off the Mosquito coast. The Earl of Warwick
was the leader in this enterprise, which maintained a colony
for nearly eleven years, when it was expelled by the Spanish.
In time this claim led to the title to British Honduras.

The process by which a corporation government developed
into a corporation colony was long and complicated.[a] Neither
Virginia nor Bermuda attained this type of government. The
chief feature of the Virginian colony was the grant of an
elective legislature by the officers of the company, while
under Puritan control. In Bermuda, the colony also secured

<hr/>

[a] See Osgood, "The corporation as a type of colonial government," Political Science
Quarterly, 1896; American Colonies in the Seventeenth Century, pp. 141-370.

a legislature, but was dominated by the company's officials. Only in Massachusetts Bay did the transplantation of the company, and its identification with the colony, develop a commonwealth out of a trading company, and amalgamate the interests of the proprietors and the colony.

The only methods by which English colonies in fact came under the direct administration of the royal officials were either conquest of a colony settled by another power, or the lapse of a charter.   Instances of both these occurrences in the early period of American colonization had marked effects upon its later history.   The lavish granting of charters came to an end for lack of sovereign power and opportunity.[a] Even before 1640, when this occured, attempts had been made to vacate the charters of both the companies that had founded mainland colonies, not from any hostility to charters themselves, but rather from opposition to the political party whose members were prominent in those corporations.   The London Company, as well as that of Massachusetts Bay, was composed of Puritan gentlemen.   The leaders of the former being more prominent, and their opposition to the royal policy more marked, it lost its charter first.   The courts were ordered to enter a writ of "quo warranto" against the patent of the London Company, and upon its successful prosecution in 1624 the colony of Virginia fell under the direct government of the King as a kind of royal proprietor.   The continuance of a legislative assembly in the colony seems not to have been intended.   On the contrary, the King wished to rule by an appointive governor and council.   But on petition from the colonists the assembly was reinstated[b]—a fact of great importance to American constitutional history.   Hereafter there was, from the standpoint of the English administrator, a new type of colonial government, that, namely, under the direct control of the Crown.   Nevertheless, no regular organs of colonial administration were yet developed, and the affairs of the royal colonies were an undifferentiated part of the business of the privy council.

The attack on the charter of the northern colony was delayed until 1635, when the "quo warranto" entered against it

---

[a] The only charter for government issued by the Parliamentary commission under the Earl of Warwick was that for Providence Plantations in 1643.

[b] Cal. Col. State Papers, I, 73, 76; Brown, First Republic in America (Boston, 1898); Mass. Hist. Colls., 4th series, ix, 89.

narrowly failed of success, and the colony, by judicious neglect, was left to develop its institutions unhindered. The Bermuda Company and the proprietaries were also unmolested for a time.

The heritage of the protectorate and of the growth of the sea power of England, was several colonies added by conquest. Jamaica, the most important of these, remained under military rule until the reign of Charles II; but plans for its organization under civil authority were drawn by the protector's statesmen, and the new King, instead of reversing these, confirmed Cromwell's governor, and instituted an assembly in 1664. The acquisition of New Netherland the same year was an unforseen consequence of the Dutch wars. It formed the connecting link between the northern and southern colonies.

POST-RESTORATION GRANTS.

With the restoration began a new series of lavish grants, both proprietary and corporation. Of all the Stuarts, Charles II was the most lordly dispenser. The newly-conquered New Netherland was granted like a royal appanage to his brother of York, the Carolinas and Bahamas to his favorite courtiers, and Pennsylvania to the powerful Quaker, William Penn. In 1662, also, the outlying colony of Connecticut, an offshoot from Massachusetts Bay, succeeded in securing a royal charter, drawn up by its agent, Winthrop, on the model of that of the mother colony; and the next year the dissenting colony of Rhode Island obtained a similar favor. The corporations thus chartered immediately became commonwealths, because the companies consisted of their own members, resident in the colonies. The companies were created for the purposes of government, and not for trade and adventure; their charters thus differed from all others yet issued, except that of Rhode Island in 1643. In 1663 that portion of the Carlisle grant which covered the Barbados was revoked at the instance of the inhabitants. Thus three colonies—Virginia, Jamaica, and Barbados—lay under the direct control of the Crown. Thenceforward until the last years of Charles II only one event involving chartered colonies need be mentioned. This was the incorporation, in 1670, of the Hudson's Bay Company, a trading concern on the Virginia model formed to exploit the great northland not yet under the dominion of any Christian prince.

The success of the greater proprietary colonies was such
that the privy council and later the Board of Trade and
Plantations were beset with petitions from persons soliciting
the grant of new fiefs.   Penn was the last individual, however, who received the grant of governmental powers.   But
mere proprietary grants were still made.   Thus in 1691, Sir
John Hoskins obtained one for the islands of Trinidad, Assun-
cion, and Martin Vaz.[a]   But the powers of government were
carefully reserved, and the charter bore no resemblance to the
earlier fief.   A similar proprietary charter was granted in
1722 to the Earl of Montague for St. Lucia and St. Vincent,
but the government was to be under the charge of the royal
governor at Barbados.[b]   In 1718 Sir Robert Montgomery
obtained a grant from the proprietors of Carolina for a large
tract of land south of that colony.   He applied to the Crown
for confirmation of his title, with the purpose of founding a
new proprietary, to be kown as Azilia.   The attorney-general
gave an opinion that the powers of government granted to
the proprietors of Carolina could not thus be divided and
alienated, and the plan came to nothing.[c]

An entirely original grant was that given to Oglethorpe for
his eleemosynary scheme in Georgia.   The governmental features of this charter were carefully guarded; laws ordained by
the trustees for the colony were subject to the royal veto; the
appointment of the governor was required to have royal
approval; after twenty-one years the province was to revert
to the Crown.

Shortly after the French and Indian war, the idea of proprietary colonies was revived for the stretch of land known
as the "back country."   The proposed colony of Vandalia
had many supporters and was about to receive a royal patent
when the troubles preliminary to the Revolution began.
Just before the Revolution, also, Richard Henderson of North
Carolina attempted to found a Kentucky proprietary known as
"Transylvania," but the title was merely based on an Indian
purchase, and quickly lapsed.   These attempts are interesting,

[a] These islands being in the possession of Spain, the proprietary grant was worthless.
Trinidad fell to the British Crown in 1802.

[b] The colony sent out was unsuccessful, and these islands continued under French
control until after the peace of Amiens (1802).

[c] B. of T. Papers, Props. Q., 146, 186. The latter paper bears upon the British attempt
to colonize at the mouth of the Mississippi. See also Rawlinson Manuscripts (Bodleian
Library, Oxford), A, 505:2.

however, as showing that whenever waste lands came within
the range of settlement the speculative temper turned at once
to the idea of founding a proprietary with the immediate right
of government.[a]

SUBINFEUDATION.

The question of succession to the rights of a proprietorship became complicated as time passed.   The laws of inheri-
tance provided for the descent of an estate, but some of the
proprietors wished to dispose of all or part of their fiefs, and
the question of subinfeudation arose.   We have seen that the
charters suspended the writ of "quia emptores," but the
question of what share of the rights and regalities might be
disposed of was a troublesome one.   The New England
council in 1623 divided all its lands into twenty parts, and
again, on its dissolution in 1635, it parceled out its vast
domain among eight members.   Only Gorges succeeded in
getting his share confirmed by .the Crown; and when the
heirs of the New Hampshire portion claimed governmental
rights, the English courts decided the case against them, and,
in 1679, the territory in question was organized into a fourth
royal province.[b]   The island of Barbados was leased by the
heirs of Carlisle to Lord Willoughby for twenty-one years,
with the rights of government included.   The English authorities not only acquiesced in Willoughby's governorship, but,
upon the revocation of the charter (1663), granted him an
indemnity for the seven years of the lease yet to run.[c]

The most noted examples of subinfeudation under a proprietary charter are those of the Jerseys and the three
counties on the Delaware.   The Duke of York, in 1664, gave
a patent for the Jerseys to Lords Carteret and Berkeley, "in
as full and ample manner as the same is granted to the said
Duke of York."   Upon this authorization the proprietors
not only assumed the powers of government for themselves,
but sold and disposed of the same.   The later forfeiture of
the proprietary rights in the Jerseys turned largely on the

---

a Turner "Western State Making," Amer. Hist. Rev., 1895; Alden, "New Governments
west of the Alleghenies before 1780," in Univ. of Wis. Bulletin, Hist. Series, ii, No. 1 (Madison, 1897). The Vandalia government was a limited proprietary; the officials were to be
paid by the company, but appointed by the Crown. Among the other proposals for colonies the corporation idea prevailed; several were to be like Massachusetts or Connecticut.
b Cal. Col. State Papers, 1677–80, No. 1045.
c This was the origin of the well-known 4½ per cent duty.

legality of their action in putting the province in the market. In spite of the fact that the Duke of York had confirmed the claims of the purchasers they were held to be without governmental rights. Delaware was in like manner indentured to Penn, by the same royal grantor, in 1682, and the proprietor of Pennsylvania had a long struggle over this portion of his vast estate.[a]

Thus we see that the seventeenth century was the great epoch of charter-granting for the purpose of planting colonies. There are two distinct periods. The first, that of the earlier Stuarts, was followed by a brief reaction, during which the charter of the London Company fell, and that of Massachusetts was attacked. No more grants were made until the Restoration, when the second period began. The reaction that followed the second period was much more marked, and attended with much greater results for the history of American institutional growth. It begins with the attack of kings Charles II and James II on the liberal institutions of the English constitution, and continued to influence the administrative policy of the home government even after the revolution of 1688.

STUART FORFEITURES.

Upon the downfall of Shaftsbury and the failure of the exclusion bill in Parliament, Charles II discerned that the centers of the opposition were the boroughs, and that while he could control the parliamentary representation of the shires through the sheriffs the municipalities were intrenched behind their charters. He also perceived that an active center of Puritan theocracy, with a church not affected by the test act, and a magistracy strictly resisting his orders, was protected by the charter of Massachusetts Bay. His attention had been called to the independent attitude of that Commonwealth immediately after his return to the throne by its action in shielding regicides. Before the conquest of New Netherland, therefore, he sent out a commission of four members to adjust the affairs of the colonies. This commission, failing to secure the consent of the Massachusetts authorities to take over appeals, made a report to the King that evoked

_a_ See Chapter II, post.

from him a stern rebuke for the recalcitrant colony, and an order to send agents to England to answer for their conduct. The policy of Massachusetts being to temporize, they replied with an address to the King; and the matter rested for ten years. In 1676 the dispute over the Mason and Gorges's claims to the territory north of Massachusetts, over which it was exercising sovereignty, became acrimonious, and it was suggested that Edward Randolph be sent over as a special agent to press the proprietary rights and to report on the condition of the colony. Randolph was received with scant courtesy by the Massachusetts magistrates; his requests and demands were ignored, and his just authority was slighted. Sorely did the colony have cause to rue the enmity of this one man. His was a mind to which system and order seemed the purpose and end of government. To his thought duty and justice consisted in scrupulous conformity to the letter of the law. He had an enthusiasm for the English system of trade, and a consistent policy of making the colonies subserve the prosperity of the mother country. Charters stood in the way of uniformity and vigor in the trade system, as well as of other measures of the English administrative policy. The simplest plan would be to get rid of the charters, when systematic management of the colonies for the benefit of England might be undertaken. Of all the colonies shielded behind charters, Massachusetts had been the most lax and culpable, both with regard to the acts of trade and to the administrative plans of the Government. Since this colony was already in disfavor with the English authorities, it would not be difficult to bring about the revocation of its charter at an early date.[a]

On Randolph's return to England after his first mission his plans were already matured for this purpose, and a series of charges was presented to the privy council and laid before the King.[b] The Massachusetts agents who had been sent over to attend to the Mason and Gorges claims were astounded. They declared that they had no authority to reply to any such charges without consultation with the officers of the colony. Meanwhile Randolph was sent back to Boston as inspector of

---

[a] In 1684 Randolph wrote, "I have worked nine years to bring the government of Boston to a regulation, and have attended the prosecution of their charter, against which judgment is now entered." Cal. Col. State Papers, 1681–85; 1931.

[b] Cal. Col. State Papers, 1677–1680, 294, 295,

customs for that port. He became involved in difficulties over the enforcement of the regulations for commerce, and was more than ever convinced of the necessity of subduing this haughty colony to the King's immediate rule.   On his return to England a second time, in order to prosecute the case against the colony, additional charges were laid.   In particular it was asserted that a number of the laws of the colonial legislature were contrary to those of England.[a] Because of the irregularities thus urged against the colony, and its inability to justify itself in the eyes of the King, who had already entered upon his opposition to the charters of the English municipalities, a "quo warranto" was issued against the charter of the company of Massachusetts Bay in 1681, and Randolph was deputed to serve the writ, at the same time being commissioned auditor and surveyor of customs for all the northern district of North America.   The case of the colony was desperate.   Its agents reported that the only choice lay between voluntary submission and the processes of the courts.   The London and Bermuda charters had been vacated by "quo warrantos," and there was no hope that Massachusetts could escape. · "It were better," replied the Massachusetts general court, "if we must die, to perish by the hands of others than our own."   Voluntary submission being thus rejected, the case was continued in the English courts.   The time limit of the writ that Randolph had served having expired on his return, the case was ordered to be entered in chancery, and in default of defense the charter of Massachusetts Bay was vacated by a "scire facias" October 23, 1684.[b]

The case of the Bermuda charter shows how entirely the attitude of a company resident in England corresponded with that of a proprietary, and how completely it contrasted with that of a corporation organized into a colony.   The inhabitants of Bermuda themselves made the complaints and entered the charges against the company.   The latter had been trying to enforce special trade regulations, requiring all tobacco to be shipped in their own vessels, and fixing the price at which

---

[a] Cal. Col. State Papers, 1677–1680.

[b] Cal. Col. State Papers, 1680–1685, 1742, 1745, 1762. Palfrey, in his History of New England (Boston, 1858–1890), III, 390, argues at some length the cause of the transfer to chancery. It would seem to have been largely a matter of form in the time required for serving the "quo warranto" writ.

it should be sold.   The planters petitioned for redress, and although the company resisted, their charter was annulled at the same time as that of London in 1683.[a]

The ground having thus been cleared for positive reorganization of colonial governments, a plan was discussed in the autumn of 1684 for a united government for all New England, and the governor chosen was Col. Percy Kirk, later of notoriety in suppressing Monmouth's Revolt.   He was to be commissioned governor of New Hampshire, which had been organized as a royal province in 1679; of Maine, which had devolved upon the Crown at the dissolution of the Massachusetts charter;[b] of New Plymouth, as " having no legal charter or constitution;" and of the lately reduced province of Massachusetts Bay.   The report continues: "Their Lo[ps]. doe likewies observe that the Colonys of Rhode Island and Connecticut are governed at present by charters, which are not yet vacated by any Proceedings at Law."   The first plan for the government permitted an assembly, which was later stricken out at the express request of the King.[c]   Kirk declined to undertake this experiment in autocratic government, and until a governor-general should be chosen Joseph Dudley was commissioned president of the council, with Randolph as secretary.[d]

As the sole hindrance to the consolidation of all New England was furnished by the charters of the two small colonies of Connecticut and Rhode Island, Randolph went out armed with "quo warrantos" to serve upon both.   The time limit for serving the writs having elapsed before his arrival in Boston, he endeavored to prevail upon these colonies to offer a voluntary submission to the King.   Rhode Island, feeling utterly unable to stand a suit at law, made a humble address to the monarch offering its government to his royal will and pleasure.[e]   The neighboring colony pursued a different plan— attempted to gain time by temporizing.   The evil day of revocation was thus put off for nearly two years, during which three "quo warrantos" were successively served against the

---

[a] Cal. Col. State Papers, 1680–1685, 1277.

[b] Ibid, 1955.

[c] Colonial Entry Book, Public Record Office MSS., 108, 21, 35. Cal. Col. State Papers, 1680–1685, 1928.   Edward Randolph, Prince Society Publications (Boston, 1898), I, 244–247.

[d] Randolph opposed Kirk's appointment and favored Dudley's. Mass. Hist. Colls., 4th series, VIII, 225; Prince Society, Edward Randolph, IV, 28. Dudley's commission is in Mass. Hist. Colls., 1st series, V, 244, but the date is incorrect; it should be September 27, 1685.

[e] Rhode Island Colonial Records (Providence, 1856–1865), III, 191.

charter and a number of addresses and remonstrances sent to the King.   Connecticut's case was complicated by the efforts of Governor Dongan to have this colony annexed to his government of New York, and in instructions to their agent the colony's general court expressed a preference for union with New England, if the integrity of the colony could not be maintained.[a]   The newly chosen governor-general, Andros, arrived in Boston December 20, 1686.   In the following March he wrote to the secretary of state that "Connecticut has not surrendered, notwithstanding another writ has been served upon them, the significance of His Majesty's pleasure and command to me for them, and their pretended loyalty and readiness to obey."[b]   But a letter which the colony had meanwhile sent to the English authorities was construed by them as a submission, and an order in council issued for Andros to take over the government.[c]   Thus the process at law against the corporation of Connecticut was suspended.   Inscribed on the Colonial Records is this significant entry: "His excellency, Sr Edmond Andross Kn^t, Capt. Generall & Govr of his Maties Territorie & Dominion in New England, by order from His Matie, James the Second, King of England, Scotland, France & Ireland, the 31 of October, 1687, took into his hands the Government of this colony of Conecticott, it being by his Matie annexed to the Massachusets and other colonys under his Excelencies Government.   Finis."

James II's policy for America was imperial in scope.   He, but lately the greatest proprietor, aimed at the abolition of all proprietary governments and the union of all the northern colonies under a single governor-general, with no legislative assemblies to obstruct his course.   Partial as he was to William Penn, it was rumored that he intended to confiscate the latter's patent and that of Lord Baltimore as well.[d]   As for the Jersey governments and that of Delaware, Randolph, on his triumphant return to America, was furnished with "quo war-

[a] Colonial Records of Connecticut (Hartford, 1852–1890), III, 222, 227, 352, 356, 368, 376, 379, 380, 463; Prince Society, Edward Randolph, IV, 97.

[b] R. I. Col. Recs., III, 233.

[c] Conn. Col. Recs., III, 222, 463; Mass. Hist. Colls., 4th series, II, 297.   The Connecticut authorities claimed that their letter "was never intended for a resignation."   See Bulkeley, People's Right to Election or Alteration of Government in Connecticut Argued (Philadelphia, 1689), reprinted in Conn. Hist. Colls. (Hartford, 1860), I, 56–81.   Fortunately for the future charter government the resignation was accepted or the process at law would have been completed.

[d] Prince Society, Edward Randolph, IV, 40, 270.

rantos" against them all.   In vain the proprietors of the Jerseys argued that they held their charters by James's own deed
of grant.   The King was inexorable, and thinking submission
more feasible than resistance, the East Jersey owners drew
up a form of surrender for their government.   Their rights
to the soil they retained.[a]   It was understood that the West
Jersey proprietors would follow suit, and a commission was
drawn for Andros as governor of New York and the Jerseys
April 16, 1688.[b]

Penn's influence with the King was sufficient to save the
counties on the Delaware, and a confirmation of his title was
drawn, and but awaited the royal signature when the revolution of 1688 began.[c]

It is interesting to speculate upon what would have been
the result for American Constitutional history had the Stuart
policy of consolidation and centralization been perpetuated.
Doubtless some mode of resistance would have been found in
America had not the English dissatisfaction broken into open
revolt in time to relieve the oppressed colonists.   Halifax's
famous defense of the Massachusetts constitution—"it was
vain to think that a population sprung from English stock
and animated by English feelings would long be deprived of
English institutions"—was a prophecy soon to be fulfilled.
Indications were not wanting of dissatisfaction and revolt
throughout the entire length of the colonies.   In Barbados
the rule of James II was much disliked.   Even as Duke of York
he had injured the islands through the Royal African Company, of which he was president; after his accession, further
taxes on sugar and the importation of political prisoners after
the Monmouth revolt had disturbed the well-being of this
rich island colony.   The disorders in the Carolinas were taxing the proprietor's patience to the utmost.   The Protestants
of Maryland, alarmed at the reprisals for Coode and Fendall's
revolt, arose at the first news of the Prince of Orange's success in England, overthrew the proprietor's government, and
excluded Catholics from all share in the government.   Even
the loyal Virginians were protesting against Effingham's
attempt to "lay taxation without representation;" to estab-

[a] Board of Trade Papers, P. R. O. MSS., Proprietus, G., 48.   Printed in New Jersey Archives (Newark, 1880–1899), 1st series, II, 26.
[b] New York Colonial Documents (Albany, 1856–1863), III, 537–542.
[c] See chapter ii, post.

lish a governor's veto on legislation, in addition to that of the Crown, and to foist an aristocratic régime upon their representative system.[a] Leisler in New York repeated the exploit of the Prince of Orange, by expelling the King's deputy governor, Nicholson, and seizing the government into his own hands. In Massachusetts the very rumor of the English invasion aroused a Boston mob, Andros and Randolph were made prisoners, and a provisional government was established on the basis of the forfeited charter.[b] The "glorious revolution" was thus heartily accepted in America, and loyalty to the new sovereigns was indisputable.

But the Stuart despotism had left its traces. Charters forfeited by process of law were not restored unchanged. A body of "King's men" had been developed in the colonies, ready to push the prerogative for the benefit that might accrue to themselves. The advantages of a consolidated administration to defend the colonies in war and to enforce the acts of trade had become evident to English eyes. The issue between the English Church and the dissenters of the colonies had been thrown into strong relief. More than this, throughout the whole period of the Restoration an administrative system, guided by able statesmen, had been gaining form and force. The colonies were drawn into the stream of administrative order and control, and the results of their closer relationship to the English executive system were soon manifest. In order to understand the effects of this developed administrative activity upon the charters and upon the colonies under their protection it is necessary to review briefly the origin of the new administrative organs and to learn their relation to colonial control.

THE PRIVY COUNCIL.

The supreme administrative body of the English system of government, so far as the colonies were concerned, was the council of the King, known for many generations as the

[a] Virginia Magazine of History (Richmond, 1894), I, 176; Hening, Statutes at Large of Virginia (New York, 1823).

[b] Andros Tracts, Prince Society Publications (Boston, 1868–1874); Prince Society, Edward Randolph, IV, 266, 268; Mass. Hist. Colls., 4th series, V, 192. It was rumored that Andros was a Papist, and even in the event of the success of the Prince of Orange would attempt to hold New England for the Stuarts,

privy council.[a] The origin of its jurisdiction in colonial affairs has been variously traced, some assigning it to that statute passed in the reign of Henry VII, known as Poynings's law, by which Ireland was definitely subjected to the continual care of the King's council. Others have seen a close analogy between the status of the Channel Islands and that of the colonies "overseas." These islands never were incorporated into the legislative and administrative system of the kingdom, but remained subject only to the jurisdiction of the royal council.[b] The Isle of Man, also, with its own parliament, and an appeal to the King in council, furnishes a strong analogy to the colonial system. But a more probable explanation of the administrative powers of the privy council over the colonies is to be found in its control of trade and in its relations with the great companies of merchant adventurers. The King had long considered the care of commerce as one of the most important functions of his council, and the early records of this body are full of regulations and orders in its behalf. As early as 1547 we find it intervening in the disputes of the company whose headquarters were in Antwerp, and refusing to permit the freemen to retain the governor of their own election.[c] Thus the rights which the council exercised over the government of colonies organized by corporations had a long-established precedent.

The pressure of business before the privy council had early led to the development of the committee system,[d] and the business of the plantations was assigned now to one now to another of these committees, standing or special, until the final organization, in 1696, of the Board of Trade and Plantations differentiated what was in theory a committee of the privy council into a special organ of colonial administration. The judicial functions of the council in hearing appeals from

[a] The first mention of this term that we have noticed is in Walter of Heminburgh's Chronicle (Rolls edition, II, p. 20), when in the reign of Edward I he speaks of an act as "ordinatumque est per regem et secretem consilium."

[b] Pike, Constitutional History of the House of Lords (London, 1894), p. 307; Pownall, Administration of the Colonies (London, 1768, fourth edition).

[c] Dasent (editor), Acts of Privy Council of England (London, 1890–1902, new series), II, pp. 545, 556.

[d] Stubbs, Constitutional History of England (Oxford, 1874-1878), II, p. 257; Acts of Privy Council, III, p. 397.

the colonial courts and taking action thereon were never transferred to the new administrative body, thus the privy council remained throughout the entire period of Amreican colonial history what it is still for the British imperial system, the final and supreme court for colonial appeals.[a]

The privy council kept in its own hands also the right of final decision on the veto of laws passed by the colonial legislatures, permitting the Board of Trade and Plantations only the power of recommending that laws be confirmed or rejected. In its right to grant charters or to issue commissions to the governors of the royal provinces, the privy council possessed the ultimate constitutional authority over all the colonies, which was limited only by the fact that these charters once issued could not be revoked without due process in the courts of the kingdom. Even Parliament, though its powers were not disputed, did not succeed in fact in revoking the charters.[b] In 1764 a decision of the courts in the case of Campbell v. Hall held that commissions issued to the governers were in the nature of charters or constitutions, and that the rights therein granted to colonists, such as the right to a local legislature, could not be revoked at the will of the privy council.[c] This decision came too late to affect the destinies of the American colonies. But these commissions had tended to take on a permanent form, and thus defined in some degree the constitution of the colonies under royal control.

The relation of the Board of Trade and Plantations to the privy council depended largely on the activity and efficiency of the board. During the periods of its prominence, its recommendations were generally indorsed without question. But even then political influence and royal favoritism made the final decision somewhat uncertain. Thus it was complained of William Penn that he boasted that he "cared naught for the lords of trade and looked elsewhere for the confirmation of his rights;" and the plans of the boards, and even those of the committee for plantations of the privy council itself were frequently overruled by the King or his secretary of state.

---

a See Chapter III, post,
b See Chapter IV, post.
c Clark, Summary of Colonial Law (London, 1834), pp. 199-201.

Throughout the century preceding the American Revolution the Board of Trade and Plantations—definitely established in 1696 and abolished in 1781—was the organ of colonial administration and the official channel of communication between the home government and the local colonial governments. It was always, however, subordinate to the privy council, of which it remained in fact as well as in theory but a committee for information and intelligence; and its function as a means of communication was shared with the secretary of state, to whom colonial communications were frequently made, and who overruled the action of the board at his pleasure.[a]

The Board of Trade and Plantations, as it was commissioned by William III in 1696, was not an absolutely new and untried means of colonial administration. Various experiments in the same direction had been made since the founding of the colonies. As early as 1634, Charles I in his attempt to "govern by council" convoked an extraordinary commission for foreign plantations, chief among whose commissioners was Archbishop Laud.[b] That this was intended as an instrument to extend royal tyranny over the colonies, a glance at the powers granted will show.[c] The power of government over the colonies was defined as the power to "make laws, ordinances, and constitutions concerning either the state public of the said colonies, or utility of private persons and their lands, goods, debts, and successions." It was empowered to remove all governors, to ordain judges and establish courts, to examine and pass upon letters patent, and to provide for the relief and support of the clergy. The disproportion between the powers granted and the results accomplished is an amusing commentary on the discrepancy between legal institutions and their actual working force.[d] The recorded acts of this commission consist chiefly in an abortive attempt to vacate the Massachusetts charter by a "quo warranto"; a proclamation forbidding emigration without their license; and the ex-

---

[a] The evils of this system of divided administration are clearly set forth by Pownall, Administration of the Colonies (London, 4th ed., 1768).

[b] Cal. Col. State Papers, 1574-1660, 177.

[c] Printed in Hutchinson, History of Massachusetts Bay, 1628 to 1775 (London, 1760-68), I, 502.

[d] There was at this time but one colony (Virginia) directly subject to the Crown.

amination and restoration to Virginia of Governor Harvey, whom the people had deposed and deported.[a]

The dangers to the colonies anticipated from this commission being averted by the struggle between the King and the Parliament, and the consequent deposition of the archbishop, colonial affairs fell into the hands of Parliament. As early as November 24, 1643, a commission for the colonies of eminent parliamentary leaders was appointed, which made Robert, Earl of Warwick, governor in chief of all the plantations in America.

After the King's execution, orders were sent to all the colonies to maintain their present governments until further advices, and as soon as possible a special commission was sent out to subject them to parliamentary control. All the orders in council for this period were signed by the council of state, directing the committee for plantations to conduct colonial affairs. During this entire period there was much experimenting with administrative organs. The Protector established a council of trade, at whose head he placed his heir, Richard.[b] The Dutch "feared [this] would have proved prejudicial to our state; but we are glad to see that it was only nominal, so that we hope in time those of London will forget they were ever merchants."

The conquest of Jamaica (1655) and the organization of its government drew forth "Overtures touching a Councill to bee erected for foreign Plantations."[c] The preamble states that the interest in the plantations is growing, that the customs are increasing, and that therefore it is of the highest importance that a select council should be established for the inspection, care, and regulation of all foreign plantations. The number of the commissioners ought not to be above five or seven, because where they are many "the chiefe things are done and oft times huddled upp by a fewe, and there is seildome that steadiness or perticular care where

---

[a] Cal. Col. State Papers, I, 209, 251, 261.

[b] Birch (editor), Collection of the state papers of John Thurloe, esq. (London, 1742), IV, 177.

[c] Egerton MSS. British Museum 2395, fo. 290. Signed, Martin Noell, one of Commissioners for Jamaica, and Thomas Povey. This was drawn up under the Protectorate, and changed for presentation after the Restoration, as "His Majestie" is substituted throughout the document for "His Highness." The handwriting appears to be that of Povey's, who was clerk of the privy council under Charles II.

more are employed than are necessary and proportionable to their busyness." The author suggests, however, that some of the principal officers of state should be added for prestige, and that the persons selected ought " by their Parts, Breeding, or Experience to be proper and adequate to the work." The advantages of such a board are evident; it may regulate and improve what already belongs to England, enhance her reputation in the Indies, dispatch public business with greater efficacy, and be particularly useful if Jamaica is retained. In case of war it can collect assistance from the other colonies "which must hereafter be brought to understand that they are to bee looked upon as united, and embodied, and that their Head and Centre is heere." Proceeding to definite enumeration of duties, the suggestors remark that at the first entrance upon their duties the councilors should write to every governor requiring exact and particular accounts of the state of their affairs and of the nature and constitution of their laws and government, and in "what modell they move;" this to be done not only to get information "but to rouse upp & advertise all Persons intrusted or concerned that His Majestie takes speciall and gracious and vigilant notice of them, and is vigilant for their general good." "This Councill is to apply all prudentiall meanes for the rendering those Dominions usefull to England, and England helpful to them, and that the severall Pieces and Collonies bee drawn and disposed into a *more certaine, civill and uniforme waie of Government; and distribution of publick Justice;* (in which they are at present most scandalously defective) And that such Collonies, as are the Propertie of perticular Persons, or of Corporation may be reduced as neare as can bee to the same method and Proportion with the rest; with as little dissatisfaction or Injurie to the Persons concerned as may bee."

The council also should settle a correspondence and be able to give an account every year of the government of each place; of its complaints, wants, and products; of every ship trading there, its lading, and whither consigned, so that the whole may be understood and the balance arranged "that soe each place within itself and all of them being as it were made into one Commonwealth, may by his Majestie bee here governed and regulated accordingly upon Common and equal

Principles." The council should also inquire into the manner in which foreign princes regulate their colonies; it should have a treasury for public defense, for the public service of the colonies, and for paying the expenses of the council. The right to summon merchants and seamen for advice and information should be allowed; and finally one person should be able to represent things to the King and council, prepare papers, receive dispatches, and keep a register.[a] This excellent and comprehensive state paper is on its face a bid for office, and it proved a successful one, since Thomas Povey became the first clerk of the council for plantations in 1660. But it is far more important as an early sketch of a uniform colonial policy to be pursued by an administrative body. In this interesting document are laid down the plans of the permanent Board of Trade and Plantations constituted forty years later.

On the organization of the administration after the Restoration, colonial affairs received fresh attention. A committee for plantation affairs, composed of ten prominent lords, was set off in the privy council on July 4, 1660,[b] and on the 7th of November in the same year a council for trade was erected.[c] Among its instructions was one ordering this council to consider and propound remedies for the inconveniences of English trade, to examine treaties and statutes to that end, concluding with directions to inquire: "How the forrange Plantations may be made more usefull to the Trade and Navigation of this Kingdome."[d] Three weeks later the first council of foreign plantations was appointed, consisting of Clarendon, Lord Chancellor, the Lord Treasurer, and forty-six other privy councilors.[e] In their instructions they were directed to inform themselves of the state of the plantations and procure copies of the grants under which they were settled to correspond with the governors and require accounts of the laws and governments from them to use means for bringing the colonies "into a more certaine, civill and uniforme way of

---

[a] Egerton MSS., British Museum, 2395, fo. 276, contains another proposal for a permanent officer or secretary "for want of which there are no records existing."

[b] Cal. Col. State Papers, I, 483. N. Y. Col. Docs., III, 30.

[c] Ibid., 30-32.

[d] Egerton MSS., British Museum, 2395, fo. 268.

[e] Patent Rolls 12 Car.. II. N. Y. Col. Docs., III, 32-34.

Government," to investigate the colonial policies of other
European states, to secure transportation of noxious and unprofitable persons to the plantations, to propagate the gospel,
and to have a general oversight of all matters relating to the
plantations.[a] The language employed indicates that the
"overtures" of Noell and Povey had been consulted and
used. The commissions for these two new councils, one for
trade, one for plantations, were renewed as their members
were changed.[b]

September 27, 1672, the two boards were united into one,
with the Earl of Shaftesbury and Lord Culpepper, as president
and vice-president.[c] This marks the advent of Shaftesbury
to political power and the appointment of John Locke as
secretary of the council.

On the downfall of Shaftesbury this policy was reversed,
and the former plan of governing by a committee of the privy
council reverted to.[d] The continued government by this committee from 1674 to 1696 may not indicate any distinct change
of policy,[e] but it is interesting as an indication of the Stuart
method of working through organs under their immediate
control, and it is worthy of remark that the despotic action of
the later Stuarts in colonial administration had for its organ
that old instrument of Stuart oppression, the privy council.

THE REESTABLISHED BOARD.

The overthrow of the last Stuart attempt at despotic rule,
and the limitation of the King's prerogative by the sovereignty
of the people in Parliament, those momentous consequences
of the years 1688 and 1689, worked themselves out slowly in
the consciousness of the English people, and it was many
years before a consistent and complete set of administrative
organs could develop through which the new principles might
act. A committee of the privy council continued to exercise

---

[a] Egerton, Colonial Policy, 75 note, finds a suggestion that a representative system was
to be introduced by adding merchants to the council. N. Y. Col. Docs., III, 34–36.

[b] That of the Council of Trade renewed October 20, 1668; October 16, 1669. Patent Rolls
20 and 21 Car., II; Council of Plantations renewed, July 30, 1670; March 20, 1671 (when
Duke of York was added). Cal. Col. State Papers, III, 135, 178.

[c] The warrant for the preparation of this commission was signed September 16, 1672;
patent passed the great seal, September 27. Cal. Col. State Papers, III, 407.

[d] Commission was revoked December 21, 1674. Patent Rolls, 26 Car. II, 9, No. 7. N. Y.
Col. Docs., III, 228.

[e] Doyle, English Colonies in America (New York, 1889), III, 194.

the active powers of government over the colonies during five
years after the advent of the Dutch prince to the throne of
England.[a] The creation of the new Board of Trade and Plantations was due not so much to the wishes of the official class
for a new administrative organ for the colonies as to the desire of the commercial class for an improvement of the trade
of the Kingdom. A perusal of the commission issued under
the great seal May 15, 1696, clearly indicates the subordina-
tion of colonial interests to those of commerce in the minds of
the designers of the new body.[b] This is borne out also by
the attempt of Parliament in December of the previous year
to establish a council of trade whose commissioners were to
be chosen by the Parliament. The King opposed the latter
part of the plan and ordered his ministers to maintain his prerogative in the matter. In spite of this, the influential Earl
of Sunderland declared for it, "which the King took exceedingly ill."[c] The new organ, it is apparent, was forced upon
the ministry by the Parliamentary majority.

The new board commissioned by the King's authority[d] was
directed to " enquire, examin into and take an Account of
the state and condition of the general Trade of England and
also of the several particular Trades in all Forreigne parts,
and how the same respectively are advanced or decayed, and
the causes or occasions thereof; and to enquire into and examine what Trades are or may prove hurtfull, or are or may be
made beneficiall to our Kingdom of England, and by what
ways and means the profitable and advantageous Trades may
be more improved and Extended and such as are hurtfull and
prejudiciall rectifyed or discouraged." They were also to
consider the subject of manufactures and how new and profitable ones could be introduced; and as a corollary to this work
they were to " consider of some proper methods for setting
on worke and employing the Poore of Our said Kingdome,
and makeing them usefull to the Publick, and thereby easeing
Our Subjects of that Burthen." Fisheries were also to be
encouraged, and new ones established.

---

a Appointed February 16, 1689, and consisting of the Lord President, Lord Privy Seal,
Lord Stewart, the Earls of Shrewsbury, Bath, and Nottingham, Viscounts Mordaunt and
Fauconberg, Sir Henry Capell, Mr. Powle, and Mr. Russell. Privy Council Register
1688-1690, 8.
b Printed in N. Y. Col. Docs., IV, 145-148.
c Cobbett, Parliamentary History of England (London, 1806), v, 977.
d Patent Rolls 7 William III, part 4, No. 7; Board of Trade Papers, Journal A, fo. 1.

It will thus be seen by an examination of the commission that the object was to establish a sort of bureau of commercial and economic specialists, who were both from the theoretical and practical point of view to endeavor to improve the "Trade of Our Kingdom of England upon which the strength & Riches thereof do in a great measure depend." That is, the mercantilists were to have an opportunity and a definite administrative body for the development of their policy. The colonial administration apparently played a secondary and subordinate part in the founding of the new board. Because the colonies were important to commerce the commissioners were likewise to inform themselves " of the present condition of Our respective Plantations as well with regard to the Administration of the Government and Justice in those Places, as in relation to the Commerce thereof. And also to inquire into the Limits, of Soyle and Product of Our severall Plantations and how the same may be improved, and of the best means for easing and securing Our Colonies there and how the same may be rendred most usefull and beneficiall to our said Kingdom of England." In furtherance of this latter design they were to inquire into the possibilities of supplying English ships with naval stores,[a] and how the staples and manufactures of England might best be disposed of in the colonies,[b] and how the colonists were to be diverted from trades and manufactures which would diminish the exports from the mother country.

The administrative work for the colonies was to be limited to examining the usual instructions of the governors; to preparing a yearly report of the governor's actions; to the recommendation of proper persons for governors, deputy governors, or councillors; and to the power to "examin into, and weigh such Acts of the Assemblies of the Plantations respectively as shall from time to time be sent or transmitted hither for Our Approbation." The commissioners were also to consider "what matters may be recommended as fitt to be

---

[a] See Lord, Industrial Experiments in the British Colonies of North America (Baltimore, 1898, Johns Hopkins University, Studies in History and Political Science, extra volume 17).

[b] Note a report of 1706: " We are humbly of opinion that the wares and merchandises of any sort to be sent from England for the supply of Your Majesty's Plantations ought rather to be recommended to your subjects there by their proper goodness, usefulness, and cheapness than be imposed on them at a fixed price by the power and compulsion of laws."   B. of T. Papers, Pl. Gen'l, Entry D, 131.

passed in the Assemblys there; To heare complaints of Op-
pressions & maleadministrations, in Our Plantations, in order
to represent as aforesaid what you in your Discretions shall
thinke proper; And also to require an Account of all Monies
given for Publick uses by the Assemblies in Our Plantations,
and how the same are and have been expended or laid out."
As an administrative body, therefore, the newly erected board
of commissioners was a means for obtaining information and
preparing advice for the direct action of the King in council.
In this fact lies the secret of its impotence and the cause
for the failure of every complete and systematic line of policy
which it attempted to carry out.   Compared with the earlier
commission under Charles I, with the Parliamentary committee of 1643, and with the council of Charles II, the powers of
the Board of Trade and Plantations under William III show
a progress in definiteness and differentiation of the organs of
colonial government, a greater knowledge of the processes at
work upon the other side of the ocean, and a more patent
determination to exploit the colonies for the benefit of England.   But on the other hand they indicate an unwillingness
to render the colonial administration independent of the control of the Crown and of its chief ministers.[a]

Constituted in this manner, the Board of Trade and Plantations assembled for its first session in Whitehall June 25,
1696.[b] William Popple was appointed secretary, a position
which he held for life and bequeathed to his descendants.
The board was to hold three meetings a week, and Sir Christopher Wren was desired to prepare rooms for its use.

The method of business was as follows: The secretary presented the matters for consideration in the shape of communications from the colonies (that is, letters from the governors;
petitions of the colonists, or of merchants residing in England); communications from the privy council or from the
secretaries of state, referred to the consideration of the board;
petitions or letters requesting nominations for colonial offices;
or communications from the commissioners of customs or of
the Admiralty asking for information and advice in matters
pertaining to their respective departments.   The quorum for

a Compare this with the final clause of the Commission of 1660, whereby the commissioners are empowered to request an extension of powers if they deem it necessary.
b B. of T. Papers, Journal A.

the transaction of business was at first 5, but shortly after it was reduced to 4.   In search of information the board issued summons to appear before them to merchants, colonial officials, and any persons knowing the conditions of the colonies.[a]   In matters of legal and constitutional difficulty the advice of the attorney-general and of the solicitor-general (either one or both) was resorted to.   The need of legal advice became so constant that in 1718 a special counsel was appointed, who advised the board in regard to matters not considered of sufficient importance to require the opinion of the high officers of the Crown.[b]   After any matter before the board had been thoroughly canvassed and discussed the secretary drew up the opinions and conclusions of the board in the form of a "representation to His Majesty in council."   This was signed by the members present and forwarded to the privy council.   All routine business was there approved at once and an "order in council" issued for the execution of the affair.   A copy of such orders was sent to the Board of Trade and Plantations and filed with their papers.   In matters of importance—recommendations of a change in policy or of unusual measure in regard to colonial administration—the proposal of the board was frequently reversed in the King's council and the plans of the board thus brought to naught.   The connection with Parliament was slight at first, only occasional requests for papers and information coming before the board, but after the Hanoverian succession and the dominance of the Parliamentarian idea the board was frequently requested to furnish complete accounts of the state of the colonies for the information of the legislative body.

This cumbrous and complicated system of reference, and the lack of authority on the part of the board are thus summarized in a representation of 1721.[c]   "The present method of dispatching business is lyable to much delay and confusion, there being no less than three different ways of proceeding herein; that is to say (1) by immediate application to Your Majesty by one of Your Secretaries of State (2) by Petition to Your Majesty in Council and (3) by Representation to

---

[a] Their commission gave them power to examine witnesses upon oath, but they do not appear to have utilized this, the testimony being optional and informal.

[b] B. of T. Papers, Journal T, April 21, 1718.   See account in Chalmers's Opinions of Eminent Lawyers (London, 1858), preface.

[c] Ibid., Pl. Genl., Entry E, 286 ff.

Your Majesty from this Board: from whence it happens that
no one Office is thro'ly informed of all matters relating to the
Plantations, and sometimes Orders are obtained by surprize,
disadvantageous to Your Majesty's service; whereas if the
Business of the Plantations were wholly confined to one Office,
these inconveniences would be thereby avoided." No change,
however, was made in this system and the board became less
and less a factor in colonial administration, until the time of
Lord Halifax, who became president in 1748, and whose aim
was to render his office independent of the secretary of state.
He obtained an agreement (1751) that the patronage and correspondence of the colonies should be vested in the board
alone; and in 1757, as president of this organization[a] he was
himself included in the cabinet. The continuance of this
arrangement depended chiefly on the influence of the person
who headed the board. In 1768 it was definitely abolished,
a third secretary of state with a cabinet portfolio being
appointed for the colonies and made an ex officio member of
the Board of Trade and Plantations.[b] The result was to
reduce that body to a "mere board of report upon reference
to it for advice or information"[c] on the part of the secretary,
and a new commission was made out to that effect. From
this time on the board sank more and more into insignificance
until it finally went down under the ridicule of Burke in
1781; and Gibbon, who was a member, could say "The lords
of trade blushed at their inefficiency, and Mr. Eden's appeal
to our twenty-five hundred volumes of reports served only to
excite a general laugh."

THE PERSONNEL OF THE BOARD.

The commission establishing a permanent Board of Trade
and Plantations declared that it should be composed of the
following great officers of state: The chancellor, president of
privy council, lord treasurer, the lord high admiral, and the
two secretaries of state. But these officers were ex-officio
members; the active members of the board were eight in number (reduced to seven in 1708), presided over by a great nobleman of the prevailing political party. During the reigns of

---

a Fitzmaurice, Life of William, Earl of Shelburne, * * * with extracts from his
papers and correspondence, 1737-66 (London, 1875-76), I, 240, 241.

b Ibid., II, 2, 3. N. Y. Col. Docs., VIII, 7.

c Life of Shelburne, II, 8.

the Orange-Stuarts the change in the president and usually
the second member of the board, who were of the government
nobility, followed the fluctuations of party rule. The first
president, the Earl of Bridgewater, and his companion, the
Earl of Tankerville, were prominent Whigs, brought into
power with the first Whig ministry. Lord Stanford, the second president (1699), was a rigid Whig who had found favor
under William III, but was deprived of all office by Anne,
until with the return of the Whigs in 1707, he was again made
president, and held the office until superseded by the Tory
Earl of Winchilsea in 1711. The third president, Lord Dartmouth, 1702–1707, was a vigorous Tory who, although deposed
from the presidency in 1707, retained his place on the board
until he became head of the ministry that brought about the
downfall of Marlborough and Godolphin (1711). At the decease of the Earl of Winchilsea in 1713, the second member,
Lord Guilford, son of the Stuart chancellor of that title, took
his place. At the Hanoverian succession an entirely new
board was formed. It was presided over first by Lord Berkeley of Stratton for about six months; then by the Earl of
Suffolk and Binden, 1715–1718; followed by the Earl of Holde-
mess, 1718–19. After this changes were comparatively few.
The Earl of Westmoreland presided from 1719 to 1735; the
Earl of Fitzwalter, 1735–1737; and Lord Monson from 1737
to 1748, when the Earl of Halifax was given the presidency.
He was succeeded by Sandys in 1761. Charles Townshend
and Lord Shelburne followed in rapid succession. Lord
Hillsborough became president from 1766 to 1772, and was
succeeded by Lord Dartmouth, who held office until the
American Revolution.

But while the fortunes of the presiding officer varied with
the rise and fall of political ministries, the active working
members of the board were seldom changed for such reasons.
The first Board of Trade and Plantations was an interesting
assembly of experts. Three of the members were diplomats
of long experience, and three others noted writers on philosophical, scientific, and economic subjects. Sir Philip Meadows,
who served the board faithfully for eighteen years, had succeeded Milton as Latin secretary to Cromwell's council; and
during his retirement, under the Restoration, had published
a work entitled "Observations Concerning Dominion and

Sovereignty of the Seas." William Blaithwait, who had been Sir William Temple's secretary at The Hague, was a prime favorite of William III, and because of his linguistic skill accompanied the King on one or more campaigns. He was an active member of the board for eleven years after its organization.[a] John Methuen, later lord chancellor of Ireland and ambassador to Portugal, was replaced in 1697 by George Stepney, who, as a poet as well as diplomat, was considered worthy of a final resting place in Westminister Abbey. Although he was often absent on diplomatic matters, Stepney's knowledge of foreign affairs made him a valuable councillor, and in more than one instance he gave direction to the board's policy. Like Blaithwait, he was a member for eleven years. But men of theory as well as of practice were deemed necessary to the exercise of the functions of the new administrative organ. Chief among these was Locke, whose age permitted him to serve but four years, but whose mental vigor made him the most energetic member during his brief tenure of office. He was peculiarly adapted to a place on the new commission, not only because of his valuable political and economic knowledge, but because of his especial interest in the colonies. As secretary to the Carolina proprietors (1669–1672) he drew up the Carolina constitutions and thought strongly of visiting America; he had also been a member of the first council of trade (1672–1674). Associated with him was John Pollexfen, a merchant and economic writer, who shortly after his appointment to office had published a "Discourse of Trade, Coyn, and Paper Credit,"[b] in which he considered labor as the sole source of wealth, and that national wealth depends on the proportion between "those that depend to have their riches and necessaries from the sweat and labor of others, and those that labor to provide those things." He was a foe of the East India Company and opposed to monopoly. Abraham Hill, the remaining commissioner, was chiefly known as a man of science and an honored member of the Royal Society.[c]

a Blaithwait had been a prominent member of the committee of trade and plantations before the revolution, and was the patron of Randolph. Much of the policy of the new board of trade and plantations is to be traced to his agency.

b London, 1697.

c His official memoranda as commissioner of trade are in Additional MSS. British Museum, 2902.

The first Board of Trade and Plantations thus constituted was by no means inactive. It was made up of men accustomed to administration and would seem to have been adapted to bring about immediate and needed reforms in colonial administration. The vigor of the first board and the notable character of the men who composed it stand in marked contrast to its later insignificance. Signs of deterioration appeared under Queen Anne, when several nobodies with great family names took the place of men of personal ability. Under the Georges, the Board of Trade and Plantations became a safe sinecure for needy members of leading families or for retired and worn-out politicians.[a] Martin Bladen, a soldier who had served under Marlborough, was made a member of the board in 1717. Until his death in 1746, he was the most vigorous of the colonial administrators, and it is said that so complete a sinecure had the position in this office become, that he was known as "Trade," because he applied himself to business, while his colleagues were known collectively as the "Board." The lack of care in keeping the records, the languor of the debates, the lapse of time between the meetings—all indicate the deterioration of the board's administration in the early Hanoverian period. This was recognized as early as 1715, when complaints were made that matters were kept too long under consideration and that persons were included in the commission "for different reasons than their ability to discharge such a trust."[b] During the first twenty years of George II's reign not only were the records badly kept but few matters of importance came before the board. Its functions were largely superseded by the committee of the privy council. Its members attended languidly, never more than two or three being present at its sessions. Under Halifax's vigorous administration a measure of energy was restored, but even then the attendance was small, and the board was swayed by the president, who was of the ruling party and changed with the shifting ministries. During Hanoverian times the most noted members, aside from the presidents, were Joseph Addison, 1715; Thomas Pelham, father and son; Daniel Pulteney, brother-in-law of the Duke of Sunderland; Charles Townshend, member in 1749, later president; and Edward Gibbon, the historian.

---

a See Horace Walpole, Memoirs. (London, 2d ed., 1847.)
b B. of T. Papers, Pl. Genl., K, 39.

THE POLICY OF THE BOARD OF TRADE.

The commissioners of trade and plantations came to their work with zeal and enthusiasm, and attempted to institute and carry out a policy for the administration of the colonies which was both consistent and definite.   Stated in brief, it was in the language of Povey's "Overtures," that the colonies "must hereafter be brought to understand that they are to be looked upon as united and embodied, and that their Head and Centre is Heere." This was no new ideal in colonial policy.   Charles I had a "full resolution" that "there maie be one uniforme Course of Government in and through our whole Monarchie," including the newly established "Collonie of Virginia;"[a] and the first council for trade and plantations was instructed to inquire into the distant dominions of foreign states "and to examine by what conduct and policies they govern or benefit them."   Aside from the Spanish and Portuguese colonies, whose mismanagement all intelligent administrators would certainly seek to avoid, the two nations that had successful colonial policies were the Dutch and the French.   One can not doubt that the policy of the Dutch had much influence during the seventeenth century. The commercialism of Dutch admin istration found its counterpart not only in the formation of English trading companies, and in the large governmental powers given them, but also in the advent of the commercial system of exploiting the colonies for the benefit of the mother country, which reached its culmination in England under the Dutch prince, William III.   The Dutch, on the other hand, were not administrators. They settled in their colonies in but small numbers, and left the control of the colonial system wholly in the hands of the large companies of merchants. The French, moreover, were the dominant people of the age. Although England and William III were engaged in breaking down that dominance, yet it is hardly to be supposed that the statesmen of that day would escape the general admiration for French methods, or fail to see the advantages of the French system of colonial administration, which was then at its best, and was making headway against the disunited, slightly gov erned English colonies. The .French ideal of a paternally governed, unitedly administered colonial state was the type

---

[a] Hazard, Historical Collections (Phila., 1792–94), I, 203.

of colonial government most in vogue and apparently most
successful.[a]

In a French treatise of the early eighteenth century,[b] after
comparing to their great disadvantage the license, independence, disobedience, and disorders of the English colonies in
America with those under French control, the author says:
" On admire à Londres la policie de nos colonies.   Il vient de
paraître un livre où elle est totalement detaillée, malgré le
fait que y est repondu sur l'objet et les epithetes injurieuses
dont on surcharge nos desseins, les plus grands louanges sont
prodiguées aux moyens que nous employons pour les faire
reussir.   Ceux qui sont à la tête de nos etablissements en
Amérique sont toujours les maîtres d'obéir, les vues de notre
Cour sont toujours uniformes, ses ordres toujours suivis.   Elle
est exactement informée de ce qui se passe, le Gouvernement
de toutes nos colonies est le même, elles ne font qu'un seul
corps.   Elles ne sont point jalouses l'une de l'autre et se
secourent mutuellement dès qu'elles en ont besoin."   This
ideal of uniformity and unity in colonial administration could
not fail to impress a body of men, brought face to face with
the practical problems of governing scattered, disunited,
heterogeneous, and often recalcitrant colonies.   The report
of 1721 but reiterates numerous previous recommendations
when it declares[c] that "The most effectual way to execute all
and render the several provinces mutually subservient will be
to put the whole under the government of one lord lieutenant
or captain-general from whom all governors shall receive
orders in all cases, who should have two councillors from
each plantation, and a fixed salary independent of the pleasure
of the inhabitants."   Such, then, was the policy of the board
of trade in the days of its vigor, and indeed throughout the
period when it may be said to have had a policy at all, to
reduce the colonial governments to one uniform type, to render them dependent upon England administratively as well as
economically, to govern them as a whole instead of as separate provinces.   What means they took to put this plan into

---

[a] The French system was the model upon which the Andros government was planned.
Some of the same administrators composed the first Board of Trade and Plantations. See
Mass. Hist. Colls., 4th series, IX, 89.

[b] Les Archives du Département des Affaires Étrangères, Paris. Mémoires et Documents
d'Amérique, Tome 22.

[c] Kings MSS., British Museum, No. 205; B. of T., Papers, Pl. Genl., Entry E, 286 ff.

execution, how far they succeeded, and why they ultimately failed, it is the province of this paper to show. What the results might have been had they succeeded is pure speculation. But it will certainly be conceded that in that event the vigor, variety, and vitality of American local government would have been stifled, the process of its adaptation to the conditions of American life would have been checked, and the emerging form of national government would have been less democratic, less American, more bureaucratic and more completely centralized.

THE SECRETARY OF STATE.

The authority of the Board of Trade and Plantations and its administrative relation to the colonies were subordinate to those of the secretary of state for the southern department, who had home and Irish affairs, as well as those of the colonies, under his control. He appointed colonial governors and other royal officers in the colonies, directed military operations therein, received and considered petitions from colonists, carried on correspondence with the governors—was, in short, the final and ultimate source of royal government, the representative toward the colonies of the Crown's prerogative. The relation between this official and the Board of Trade and Plantations rested upon his personal consideration for that body. The acts of the colonial legislatures were required to be submitted to the board, but in other matters the courtesy or choice of the secretary and customary usage governed his action. In the times of the board's vigor almost every colonial matter of importance was referred to it by the secretary. But in case of conflict of opinion the latter's will prevailed. It has already been shown how this neutralized the action of the board and prevented the carrying out of a definite policy of colonial administration. In 1752 the board procured an "order in council" directing that in the future governors should correspond with it alone, except in cases requiring His Majesty's immediate direction, such as affairs with any foreign colony or State or those concerning war.[a] But this order was dropped in 1763 and completely reversed in 1766.[b] On the

---

[a] Printed in N. Y. Col. Docs., VI, 753, 754.
[b] Ibid., VII, 848.

appointment of a secretary of state for the colonies in 1768 all colonial business passed into his hands. The proposal for a third secretary was a sign both of the aroused interest in the colonies, and a determination to centralize and fix the responsibility in their affairs directly in the hands of an officer responsible to the King.

COMMISSIONERS OF CUSTOMS.

This office became necessary after the first navigation acts went into effect and the commissioners were intrusted with collection of customs both in England and the colonies. The first board was established in 1663, and in 1670 the office was still further centralized by the appointment of a receiver-general of customs.[a]   After the revolution of 1688, the system again reverted to a board of commissioners, who took an active part in colonial affairs. They dictated many of the instructions issued to the governors, those which later served as a model being drawn up by them in collaboration with a committee of the privy council in 1686.[b]   From time to time, as new acts were passed or new exigencies arose in their enforcement, these instructions were added to at the suggestion of the board of customs.[c]   Their direct connection with the colonies was through the governors, who were instructed to correspond with the commissioners, and to send them, every three months, lists of clearances, and also reports of illegal trading. The governor's agent in matters of trade was the naval officer whom he was empowered to appoint, but who was required by the 7th and 8th William III to give security to the commissioners of customs. The chief agents of the customs board, on the other hand, were the collectors of customs whom they appointed for every port, and the surveyors-general of customs, of whom there were two for America—one for the southern and one for the northern department. Through these officers continual complaints of illegal trading were sent to the commissioners in England, and thence reported to the secretary of state, to the board of trade, and even to Parliament.

<hr>

[a] Hall, History of the Custom Revenue in England, (London, 1892), 189.

[b] B. of T. Papers, Pl. Genl. Entry F, 253.

[c] The commissioners of customs also had the right, according to 25 Charles II, to erect ports in the plantations. B. of T. Papers, Props. Entry A, 167.

THE LORDS OF THE ADMIRALTY.

The sole power of the Admiralty of England, with reference to the colonies during the early colonial period, was that of issuing to the royal governors commissions as admirals of the plantations. The governor, in consequence, might erect an Admiralty court when necessary, in which he frequently acted as judge. But with the increasing growth of trade between England and the colonies, and the greater stringency of its regulations, a need arose for courts in which to try seizures for violations of the acts of trade that should be as independent as possible of colonial prejudice and whose judges should be appointed by the King's officers in England. A provision was therefore inserted in the 7th and 8th William III by which breaches of the law were to be tried, at the option of the officers, in the colonial courts or the courts of vice-admiralty. This led to the erection of such courts in all the plantations, the officers of which—judges, marshals, and registers—were chosen and commissioned by the Board of Admiralty in England.[a]

The struggle, therefore, of the common-law courts with the Admiralty jurisdiction, which had raged so strongly in England in the sixteenth and seventeenth centuries,[b] was transferred to the colonial arena, where the opposition was intensified by colonial prejudice against all King's officers and the question complicated by the double jurisdiction of the governors and the judges. Complaints to the Lord High Admiral[c] or the judge of the Admiralty were constant, and were referred in many cases to the secretary of state, to the board of trade, and even to Parliament. These vice-admiralty courts in the plantations constituted an intercolonial judiciary, which acted without juries, was independent of colonial control, and dependent upon the Admiralty in England. By attempting to draw an increasing number of cases within its jurisdiction it operated to increase the prerogative. Its influence on the formation of the Supreme Court of the United States has been often noted.[d]

---

[a] The Lords of Admiralty were not in favor of this project, which was part of the system planned by Edward Randolph. They declared that their commissions to the governors as vice-admirals were sufficient. (See post, chapter 3.)

[b] Benedict, Admiralty Practice in the United States (third edition), preface.

[c] Under William III this office was placed in commission.

[d] Jameson, "Old Federal Court of Appeal," Am. Hist. Assn. Papers (New York, 1889), III.

COLONIAL AGENTS.

A special link in the administrative system, of growing importance as the colonial policy developed, was the colonial agency. This office, evolved at first from special and urgent necessities of the colonies themselves, proved so useful and so important that the English administrators insisted on its perpetuation. The agency of Franklin gave some reason to hope that this system might have developed into some form of colonial representation in England, but it went down in the storm of the American Revolution.

As far as the English administration was concerned, the position of the agent was unofficial; but by custom and courtesy he was recognized by all administrators. Upon receiving authorization from the colony he presented his credentials to the secretary of state and to the Board of Trade and Plantations, and held himself in readiness for summons at any time. The development of the temporary and extraordinary agencies of the seventeenth century, insisted upon at times by the English Government,[a] into the permanent agencies of the eighteenth century was chiefly due to the exigencies of the charter colonies. In the long period during which their charters were imperiled they found it necessary to have some influential person present in England whose voice might be heard in their behalf. So efficient were these agents, especially those of the Connecticut colony, that their efforts defeated at two critical moments the blows leveled at the charters.

A permanent resident agent at court appealed to the provincial colonies, who rapidly adopted the system, thus showing the influence of institutions evolved by the charter colonies. In the provincial colonies control of the agent was often an object struggled for between the executive and people. The assemblies ultimately secured it, but many royal governors retained private agents of their own at the English court. In the corporate governments the agent always represented the popular party. In the proprietary colonies he served to appeal to the Crown for support in any popular struggle against the proprietors. Thus the assembly of Maryland, after first refusing to continue the agency established under

a During the struggle over the first charter of Massachusetts Bay one of the complaints against the colony was that it refused to send agents, as the privy council demanded.

royal control, were later denied by the proprietor the right to reestablish it except under nomination by himself.[a]

The agent thus was a kind of popular colonial representative. The position was usually held by some Englishman of legal attainments and political influence and connections, who had large interests, either commercial or through religious sympathy, in the colonies. Thus Sir Henry Ashurst, agent for Connecticut and Massachusetts, was the leader of the Puritan party in England; Richard Partridge, for thirty years agent of Rhode Island and New Jersey, was a Quaker by conviction. Later it became more popular to secure some American resident in England, or to retain some Parliamentary leader in the colonies' behalf, and we have Franklin and Burke as the great exemplars of colonial agents. While, therefore, the function of the agent was, from the standpoint of the English administrators, extra-official, his importance was conceded, and his appointment even required as a means of information. He served as a definite representative of colonial interests and affairs.[b]

SUMMARY.

The administrative measures of the English Government in relation to the colonies were of slow growth, the result of much experimentation. During the seventeenth century they were gradually taking form. By the beginning of the eighteenth century they had assumed a somewhat permanent shape, and entered upon a period of activity and efficiency. Under the Whig control in the reign of George II their ineptitude was marked and the conflicting features of the system were brought out in relief. After the middle of the eighteenth century a new system was tried, more highly centralized and more directly responsible than the old. But the American colonies, grown restive under the increasing supervision and interference by the home government, threw off the yoke of the mother country. The American Revolution changed the English colonial administrative system, which, since that event has adjusted itself to the exigencies of the situation, and developed into the present imperial union and federation, with home administration only as an expedient for colonies not sufficiently developed for a local autonomy.[c]

---

[a] Sharp Correspondence, Maryland Archives, I, p. 401.

[b] See Tanner, " Colonial Agents," in Political Science Quarterly, 1901, p. 24.

[c] On modern English colonial administration, see Reinsch, Colonial Government (New York, 1902).

Chapter II.

TREATMENT OF INDIVIDUAL COLONIES.

Colonial status after Revolution of 1688—New England colonies— Jerseys lose their charters—Penn's difficulties—Carolina charters canceled—The Bahamas.

COLONIAL STATUS.

When the committee for plantations of the privy council began to examine the condition of affairs at the close of the Revolution of 1688 and the restoration of stable government, the status of the plantations was found to be as follows: All the northern colonies, except Pennsylvania, had been consolidated under one governor. He had been deposed by a popular uprising in Boston, where the colonists had resumed their former government. His deputy in New York was suspended. The charters of Rhode Island, Connecticut, and the Jerseys, not having been vacated by law, became operative once more. New York and New Hampshire, as royal provinces, were subject to the Crown. The status of Plymouth and Maine was undetermined. Massachusetts Bay, having lost its charter, had no legal status. Turning to the south, we find the proprietorships in the Carolinas and the Bahamas unchanged. But, owing to disturbances, and a petition of the inhabitants, the Leeward Islands were presently (1689) taken under royal protection. William Codrington was commissioned governor and authorized to call an assembly. The difficulties incident upon the revolution in Virginia were speedily adjusted, and Francis Nicholson, late of New York, was commissioned governor of the "Old Dominion." The revolution in Maryland, having taken place in the name of the Protestant sovereigns, and the legal proprietor thereof being a papist, a royal governor was commissioned for this province, and the attorney-general was ordered to enter a writ of "scire facias" against the charter of Lord Baltimore.   No judgment was ever entered in this case, but the crown government was maintained until 1715, in spite of frequent petitions from the legal heirs of Baltimore; then the proprietor, having embraced the Protestant faith, was permitted to again resume his proprietorship unquestioned.   The colonies which needed immediate attention were those of New England.   Later the proprietary governments in the Jerseys, Pennsylvania and Delaware, the Carolinas, and the Bahamas came in for their share of regulation.

NEW ENGLAND.

At the close of the Revolution an attempt was made to restore the charters of the colonies, together with those of the English municipalities.   In the list of grievances drawn up by the convention Parliament, it was resolved that "the late prosecution of 'quo warrantos' against the cities, two universities, the towns corporate, boroughs, cinq ports, and plantations, and judgment entered thereupon, and the surrenders of charters to the violation of their ancient rights are illegal and a grievance," and in the following parliament a bill was introduced to the effect that "Whereas in pursuance of a wicked design to subvert the constitution of the English government and the Protestant Religion and to introduce arbitrary power and Popery, endeavors have been used to destroy Bodies Politick & Corporate in the Kingdom of England and Wales * * * and ye same wicked design hath been further pursued by destroying Charters, Rights, Liberties and Privilidges of the several Plantations and Colonies in New England and other parts beyond seas * * * and Quo Warrentos and Scire Facias brought against said Bodies Politick, All these surrenders are hereby declared null and void."[a] This bill passed the House of Commons, but failed in the House of Lords for lack of time, an unexpected dissolution accompanying the king's departure to settle affairs with James in Ireland.[b] The new king opposed the measure, which was therefore not reintroduced, and the restoration of corporation privileges proceeded one by one.   London received its charter again May 24, 1690.   Petitions were made at the same time

---

[a] The act was designated one " For restoring Bodies Politick and Corporate and confirming their Laws and Liberties."   B. of T. Papers, Pl. Genl., BB, 6.

[b] See a letter from Mather, Mass. Hist. Coll., 4th series, V. 254.

for the New England colonies, with every hope of a successful issue. Mather and Phips, the Massachusetts agents, presented a petition that the latter colony, those of New
Plymouth, Connecticut, and Rhode Island, should have their
respective charters restored.[a] The matter was discussed in
the privy council, and it was decided that a governor should
be sent over in Andros's place with a provisional commission,
and that such an establishment should be prepared for the
future as would "reserve such a dependence on the Crown as
shall be thought requisite."[b] At the same time it was intimated that the administration wished the charges against the
late governors dropped, and Randolph was promoted to the
position of surveyor-general of customs. Connecticut then
sent over an agent who succeeded in obtaining an opinion
from the attorney-general that since the colonial charter never
had been vacated by legal process and the submission of the
government by the authorities had been forced, that instrument was still valid.[c] Three years later the Rhode Island
agent secured a similar opinion;[d] and these two small corporation colonies, having already resumed their former governments, maintained them unchanged until the American
Revolution.

The decisive answer received by the Massachusetts agents
refusing the restoration of the former charter, and the existence in the colony of a strong party that did not favor its
resumption[e] led to negotiations for a new charter. In January, 1691, the agents requested a reestablishment of their
corporation, but stated that they were willing to accept a new
charter, and asked for propositions from the committee of
trade and plantations. The latter asserted that they were
unable to proceed until the "King had declared whether it
was his pleasure to have a governor or representative of his
own appointment. or whether he would leave the power of
making laws wholly to the people and the officers chosen by
them."[f] The reply of the King was emphatic and unequivo-

---

[a] Printed in Mass. Hist. Colls., 4th series, VIII, 705.

[b] Privy Council Register, 1688–1690, 21.

[c] Opinion rendered August 2, 1690. Printed in Hinman, Letters from the English Kings
* * * to the governors of Connecticut (Hartford, 1836).

[d] B. of T. Papers, New England, Entry 1692–1696, fo. 126.

[e] Petitions were presented, one entitled "Merchants and inhabitants of Boston," with
over 250 signatures, in opposition to a restoration of the old charter. B. of T. Papers,
Journal 7, fo. 7.

[f] Ibid., fo. 10.

cal. He declared in council that he was resolved to send a governor of his own appointment, as in Barbados and the other plantations.[a] The attorney-general was thereupon ordered to draw up a charter upon this basis.[b] From this time until the final order for the charter to pass the great seal (September 17, 1691), the agents were in treaty with the attorney-general and the lords of the committee to obtain as favorable terms as possible. The parties came to a deadlock on July 30 and the points at issue were referred to the King in person. The agents insisted that the appointment of judges, justices of the peace, and sheriffs ought to be in the general assembly, and that the governor should have no negative voice in their election.[c] The King supported the prerogative and the agents were obliged to acquiesce, their only triumph being the confirmation of the titles to land granted by the previous government and the inclusion of Maine, Plymouth, and Nova Scotia within their boundaries.

The temper of the new administration was shown not only by insistence on the great points of a royal governor with appointing and veto power, but also by the attention given to preserving the King's prerogative in lesser matters. Appeals and admiralty jurisdiction were reserved for the Crown, as well as the right to annul all laws.[d] The clergy were deprived of their political power by the change of the franchise from church members to freeholders. Limited as the charter was, the Massachusetts agents made much of their triumph in securing it, and of their success in obtaining the territory of New Plymouth and likewise that lying to the north, of which they had been deprived upon the revocation of the first charter.

In 1720-21 an acrimonious debate arose in Massachusetts over the right of the house to choose its own speaker, and to prorogue itself at will without the governor's consent. The board of trade drew up and forced upon the legislature for its consent an explanatory charter which decided both points in favor of the governor. In 1725 the privy council declared that "if such Explanatory Charter shall not be accepted and a just

a Privy Council Register, 1690–1692, Apr. 30, 1691.

b B. of T. Papers, Journal 7, fo. 15, May 12, 1691.

c B. of T. Papers, Journal 7, fo. 37; Privy Council Register, 1690–1692.

d In the first draft of the charter, laws were to be valid if not disallowed by the King within one year. The committee insisted on having this increased to three years.

regard showed to your Majesty's royal prerogative by the
House of Representatives for the future in all particulars aforesaid, it may be proper for the consideration of the legislature
[i. e., Parliament] what further provision may be necessary to
support and preserve Your Majesty's just authority in said
Province and prevent such presumptious invasion for the
future." [a] The Massachusetts assembly decided to submit and
"dutifully" accepted the curtailment of its privileges rather
than hazard the continuation of its form of government.   In
spite of the legal barriers thus interposed, the independent
spirit in Massachusetts continued to struggle against English
administrative dictation, employing methods which will be
noted in connection with those of other colonies.

THE JERSEYS.

The close of the Revolution of 1688 found the two small
provinces south of New York in much confusion.   The problem of proprietary rights was a complicated one.   Berkeley had sold his share to a stock company in 1673.   The
Cartaret share had been put up at auction in 1680, and was
bought in by a board of 24 associates, chiefly Quakers, who
secured a confirmation of their title from the Duke of York
in 1682.   Under these titles the Jerseys had a proprietary
government until forcibly annexed to New York (1688), as
we have seen.[b] After the Revolution the towns fell back
upon their local government.   Meanwhile some of the proprietors attempted to sell their rights, including the power of
government.[c] The committee for trade and plantations, "on
consideration of the great disorders the Countrys of East and
West New Jersey have a long time lain under," concluded to
incorporate them in the government of New York, and a commission to that effect was drawn up and approved by the
attorney-general.   Daniel Cox, however, petitioned to preserve his rights, whereupon these colonies were omitted from
the final draft of the commission and reserved for later consideration.[d]

---

[a] Privy Council Register, May 29, 1725.   Printed by Palfrey, History of New England,
IV, 452–454.

[b] See ante, Chapter I.

[c] Cox, chief proprietor of West Jersey, offered "the hereditary or perpetual government of West Jersey" for sale, saying, "I have refused 1,000 guineas for this only."
Rawlinson MSS. (Bodleian Library, Oxford), C, 128, 39.

[d] Privy Council Register, 1690–1692, fos. 328, 336.

Meanwhile the proprietors of both Jerseys commissioned and sent as governor a Scotchman, Andrew Hamilton, who had been deputy governor of the same colonies under Andros. He seems to have been an able and vigorous administrator, who restored order in the provinces, and, although probably still a Jacobite at heart, was quite acceptable to the majority of the inhabitants.[a] A doubt having arisen whether Hamilton, as a Scotchman, was eligible as governor of a plantation, particularly after the passage of the navigation act of 1696, barring Scotch ships, a few of the proprietors of East Jersey granted a new commission to Jeremiah Bass.[b] The latter stirred up disaffection and discord, and while pretending to serve the interests of his principals was secretly trying to undermine the proprietors' interests, and in connection with Randolph to destroy the charters.[c] The inhabitants of East Jersey refused obedience to the new appointee, and the proprietors secured an opinion from the attorney-general that Scotchmen were eligible, whereupon they reinstated Hamilton and applied for his confirmation by the King.[d]

Meanwhile the title of the proprietors to the government of the Jerseys was called in question on other grounds. A dispute arose between East Jersey and New York in regard to ports and customs duties. Perth Amboy was the port of entry for East Jersey, but the customs officers at New York required all ships that entered the bay to pay the duties laid by the latter province for its defense. The Jersey inhabitants, feeling wronged, petitioned the commissioners of customs in England for redress, and the matter was referred to the board of trade. The question at once arose by what authority ports were established. Was this a royal prerogative? Had it been included in the Duke of York's grant? Had it passed from him to the proprietors of the Jerseys? The attorney-general and the solicitor-general decided that the right to establish ports in the plantations was vested in the commissioners of customs, and that the Jersey proprietors had no grant of such a power.[e] Whereupon the board of

a See Bass's accusations that he drank "King James's health." B. of T. Papers, Props. F. 47.

b New Jersey Archives, 1st series, II, 176, 177.

c B. of T. Papers, Props. C. 29.

d Ibid., Props. 1697, 669, 679, 756. New Jersey Archives, 1st series, II, 250, 251, 257.

e Ibid, Entry A, 167. New Jersey Archives, 1st series, II, 182.

trade represented to the King that the Jerseys ought not to be allowed a port.[a] The King approved and gave orders accordingly December 29, 1697. Acting on this decision, Lord Bellomont seized the ship *Hester* (November, 1698), riding at anchor in the harbor of Perth Amboy, for not entering and clearing at New York. The proprietors again petitioned the King for redress, claiming that no notice was given them of the former order and offering, if they were allowed a port of their own, to obtain an act of assembly imposing the same duties as New York and for the same purpose.[b]

The board of trade immediately seized the opportunity to investigate the proprietors' title to the government. April 3, 1699, the proprietors wrote that they were "much surpriz'd at the Objection Yo.[r] Lord[pps] make to their Right of Government." They rested their claim on the confirmation by the Duke of York in 1682, and on the hearing at the privy council in 1692, when their government was exempted from inclusion in that of New York.[c] They offered, however, to try their right to a port by a feigned issue in the courts. The board of trade suggested including their right of government in the same trial, but to this the proprietors objected that "they can not without injustice to themselves and the inhabitants submit their right of government to such an issue."[d] The board next summoned such of the West Jersey proprietors as were in London to prove their title to the government of that province. Thereupon they admitted that their title was poor, but plead that they governed "ex necessitate rei," and begged that the King should grant them a new charter of incorporation as not "departing with anything now in the Crowne, but only a confirmation of what was formerly granted out of it." Annexation to New York, they declared, would ruin the province. The welfare of the colony and "not an Ambition of Govern[mt] induces the proprietors to desire a new grant."[e]

But the attitude of the board was inexorable, and the proprietors concluded it would be the part of wisdom to make

---

a Privy Council Register, 1697–1699, fo. 139.

b B. of T. Papers, Props., Entry A, 374. March 13, 1699.

c Ibid, Props. C., 4. New Jersey Archives, 1st series, II, 265.

d Ibid, Journal C, 439; D, 7; Props., Entry A, 400, 401. New Jersey Archives, 1st series, II, 266, 268.

e Ibid, Props. C., 24.

such terms with the central authority as they could.   Accordingly the East Jersey proprietors drew up a form of surrender July 5, 1699, in which they declared themselves ready, if thirteen conditions were complied with, to yield the government, although that " was the Cheifest motive of purchasing the said Province."ᵃ

The reply of the board was not returned to the proprietors until November 28.   Meanwhile, all general instructions and directions were withheld from the Jerseys, lest " the proprietors should, from the Direction of such a letter, infer anything to their advantage and his Majesty's prejudice."ᵇ   In the answer finally given, the board agreed to confirm to them the soil, to give to them sole rights of purchase from the Indians, to grant separate courts to East Jersey, provided the officers were appointed by the king's governor, to permit a sixth of the assembly and council of New York to be inhabitants of East Jersey (the project was to unite the province with New York), which, with another sixth granted to West Jersey, would give these provinces a fair proportion in the New York government.   The proprietors were also to be permitted to maintain courts baron and courts leet on their own lands, to grant markets and fairs, and to have the reversion,of traitor's goods and of treasure trove.ᶜ   But the chief matter in dispute was the establishment of a port.   To that condition of the proprietors the board had replied that a port at Perth Amboy might be granted, but it was " improper to bind his Majesty " in this regard.   The proprietors replied, January 15, 1700, that they were surprised at the dubious answer to this proposition, as obtaining a port to be continued forever was the main inducement for them to consent to a surrender.   " This is the only Thing that can make the Province of any value to the Proprietors, or give them hopes of reimbursing their Purchase-money and other expenses in Improvements; and if your Lordships think this is too great a privilege * * * the Proprietors cannot be accessary to their own ruine by a voluntary surrender."ᵈ   In order to secure a port of entry the proprietors endeavored to have their right to such confirmed

ᵃ B. of T. Papers, Props. C., 23.   New Jersey Archives, 1st series, II, 294.

ᵇ B. of T. Papers, Pl. Genl., Entry B., 61.

ᶜ Ibid., Props. Entry B, 133.   Printed in Smith, Hist. of New Jersey, Appendix.

ᵈ Ibid., Props. Entry B, 147, New Jersey Archives, 1st series, II, 308.

by an act in Parliament, and a petition brought in to that effect stopped the negotiations with the board of trade.[a]

Meanwhile, Bass, after ineffectual efforts to maintain himself in his governorship in opposition to Hamilton, came over to England and addressed himself to securing the unconditional confiscation of the East Jersey charter.[b] He presented a petition of one hundred and twenty-two inhabitants of East Jersey, containing complaints against the proprietors.[c] They submitted an answer alleging that the petition was the work of a faction who desired to be free from quitrents. They said that some planters had of late advanced the notion that in the Indian natives rests the sole ownership of the soil. If this doctrine should prevail all the crown grants would be royal frauds and the right of the king to govern might also be questioned. In conclusion they declared that both they and the proprietors of West Jersey had, before this complaint arrived, unanimously agreed to surrender the government of both provinces to the king under conditions proper to preserve their civil rights.[d] The board, however, was now deep in preparation for the bill of 1701, and ignored this offer of the proprietors.[e] On the failure of that bill, which Bass was largely engaged in forwarding, and by which he hoped to profit,[f] he called the attention of the board of trade to the Jerseys by again presenting, in opposition to Governor Hamilton, a petition of a number of inhabitants which declared that the governor could hold courts only by force of arms.[g] It was true that disorders had been increasing in these provinces, and had been encouraged by disputes among the proprietors. Bass's party, in the East Jersey council, had left their seats, refused to recognize the jurisdiction of the courts, rescued a pirate—one of Kidd's crew—seized the governor and justices, and imprisoned them for some days. In West Jersey they had stirred up a riot in Burlington in March, 1701, on the occasion of a tax levy.

---

[a] B. of T. Papers, Journal B, 369. February 12, 1700.

[b] Bass could not even consolidate the interests of those opposed to the Quakers. Lewis Morris, a strong Churchman, supported Hamilton.

[c] B. of T. Papers, Props. F, 42. November 5, 1700. New Jersey Archives, 1st series, II, 322–327.

[d] Ibid., F, 50. New Jersey Archives, 1st series, II, 344–353.

[e] See Chapter IV, post.

[f] Letter of Bass. Additional MSS. (British Museum), 9747, fo. 38.

[g] B. of T. Papers, Props. G, 23.

After Bass had abandoned the province and gone to England to seek redress, the party who supported him in the board of proprietors sent over Capt. Andrew Bowne, commissioned by only six of their number and without the knowledge of the others.[a] He continued to foment the discord. Hamilton's party had seen that their only hope lay in sending some one to England to counteract the representations of Bass; so, in the summer of 1701, Mr. Lewis Morris arrived to endeavor to secure Hamilton's appointment as royal governor when the surrender, which seemed imminent, should be consummated.[b] The scene of the dispute was thus transferred from the proprietors to the board of trade. In the midst of it the proprietors of both East and West Jersey presented new terms of surrender, this time stipulating that they should be erected into a separate province and not be annexed to New York.[c] After numerous hearings of both parties the board of trade presented a representation to the king, October 2, 1701, rehearsing the entire case.[d] They were satisfied that the patents of the Duke of York were not, nor could be, of any validity to convey the right of government, "which is a power inalienable from the person to whom it is granted, and not to be assigned by him unto any other, much less divided, subdivided, and conveyed from one to another as has been done in the present case." They advised that the King commission a governor at once, but also that he should obtain from the proprietors articles of surrender to their pretended right of government. In a later representation they say that reducing this province to an orderly government under the Crown "will be of good influence throughout the other plantations.[e] The proprietors agreed with the board on the instructions to be given the royal governor to protect their property interests, and signed the form of surrender April 15, 1702.[f] They could not, however, agree on the recommendation of a governor, and the board finally decided to nominate some person wholly unrelated to the factions. So

---

a B. of T. Papers, Props. G, 28.

b Morris carried with him eight proxies for the proprietors resident in the Jerseys, to be used in the surrender. B. of T. Papers, Props. G, 46.

c Ibid., G, 29. New Jersey Archives, 1st series, II, 404.

d Ibid., Entry C, 244. New Jersey Archives, 1st series, II, 420–427.

e Ibid., 39.

f B. of T. Papers, New Jersey, A, 1. Printed in New Jersey Archives, 1st series, II.

Cornbury, who was about to go to New York, was commissioned governer of New Jersey also. Hamilton, who had really governed well until the troubles fomented by Bass, was dispossessed by the enmity of the King's party, Quary and Randolph opposing his reappointment.

Thus the Jersey proprietorships were vacated and the Quaker party in these colonies defeated. Incidentally, also, the right of subinfeudation of the powers of government by transfer and sale was denied, and the peril of indefinite subdivision and multiplication of proprietary governments avoided.

PENNSYLVANIA AND DELAWARE.

William Penn was a sturdy and declared Jacobite, and had been an especial favorite of James II. After the revolution, however, he refused to flee, as solicited to do by his friends. He was therefore arrested on charge of treason, committed to the Tower, and his right to Pennsylvania declared forfeited. After his release on bail he endeavored to secure his proprietorship, but the committee for trade and plantations, alleging as reasons the absence of the proprietor from the province and the danger from the French, determined to include Pennsylvania with New York, and in 1692 drew up a commission for Colonel Fletcher, governor of New York, to take over the Pennsylvania government. Fletcher sent his deputy to Philadelphia, who ruled there for two years.

Meanwhile Penn had recovered from his difficulties. He was permitted a hearing in the privy council, whereat he proved that his charter was still inviolate, and Fletcher's commission consequently illegal. The council agreed to revoke this commission on condition that Pennsylvania should furnish a quota for the New York militia or its value in supplies.[a] Whereupon the proprietary government was quietly reassumed by its grantee and its title not again called in question.

But on the failure of the bill of 1701, introduced in pursuance of the avowed policy of the board to secure as many colonies as possible to the direct government of the Crown, negotiations were begun for the purchase of Pennsylvania. Penn was ready to part, for a proper consideration, with the troublesome privilege of governing a protesting province, and all

a Privy Council Register, Aug. 3, 1694.

the more willing since he had narrowly escaped losing it without remuneration, and since it was to be feared that the attempt
in Parliament would be renewed. The enmity to Penn of
Quary and the Church of England party in the colony was
persistent, and their influence with the board of trade enabled
them to make it effective.[a] The practical difficulties of any
proprietor, however just and however willing to yield to the
wishes of his colonists, were necessarily great when facing a
turbulent, eager democracy, and standing between them and
the demands of the home government in regard to trade.
Such conditions made Penn consider the burden of government heavier than its advantages and suggested overtures for
its surrender. Accordingly, May 11, 1703, he wrote to the
board of trade that, upon a just regard of his security and that
of the people in their civil rights, he would resign the government for a consideration.[b] The Queen having signified her
willingness to treat, Penn submitted "Proposals for surrender," as follows:[c]

First. Pennsylvania to continue a distinct province.

Second. The laws and constitutions to be confirmed by the
Queen except such few as he himself would object against.

Third. A patent to be given him for the lands of the three
lower counties on the Delaware.

Fourth. Thirty thousand pounds and a half-penny grant
upon the tobacco of the province.

Fifth. The right to present two persons in nomination for
governor for the choice of the Queen.

Sixth. No appeals in cases less than £200.

Seventh. Confirmation of his rights in the soil to himself
and heirs.

These conditions were too exorbitant to be considered. The
perpetual nomination of the governor would restrict the English administration in the most vital part and the whole matter was dropped. In January, 1705, Penn's second set of
proposals[e] evoked some pertinent queries from the Board, the
answers to which are interesting.[d] The chief conditions were

---

a See Chapter IV, post.
b B. of T. Papers, Props., L, 28.
c Ibid., 35, 38.
d This paper is missing; its contents are to be inferred from the succeeding one.
e B. of T. Papers, Props., N. 1.

the exemption of his heirs from taxation and the protection
of the rights and privileges of the Quakers. He also proposed
nominating three persons from among whom the royal governor should be chosen, but on objection he gave up that point.
In response to an inquiry as to what he meant by "liberty of
conscience," he replied: "I mean not only that relating to
worship but to education or schools, a coercive or ministerial
maintenance, and the militia;" and he continued, "The Quakers having founded a country of their own will be very uneasy if made dissenters therein." His proposals were not
only that Quakers should be eligible to all the offices save that
of governor, but that their marriages should be legalized,
that they should be protected "against abuse and reproach
for way of dress," and should not be obliged to serve in the
militia. The governor was to take an oath to that effect.
During all the year of 1705 Penn was in constant negotiation
for the surrender, and seemed to be on the very eve of accom-
plishing it when the troubles with Rhode Island and Connecticut culminated in the bill of 1706 and defeated his chances.[a]
In January, 1707, Penn revived the matter. The Secretary of
State wrote to the Board in favor of purchasing the right of
government to Pennsylvania, saying that he thought an equita-
ble allowance ought to be made but the surrender should
be unconditional and absolute.[b] This time Penn demanded
£20,000, of which £5,000 should be paid from the treasury
and the rest by grant from Pennsylvania. But while negotiations were pending, the Fords, Penn's agents, interfered to
secure their rights in the case at issue between them and Penn
and the matter was dropped for the third time.[c]

Meanwhile anxiety and confusion over this matter was
great in Pennsylvania. The Germans feared their naturali-
zation act would not be confirmed if the Queen assumed the
government and petitioned for favor;[d] Logan represented to
Penn that the need of the surrender was urgent and that it

[a] B. of T. Papers, Props., 30, 33, 42, 43, 49, 50, 56, 57; Journals I and K.

[b] B. of T. Papers, Props., Entry E, 439.

[c] Shepherd, History of Proprietary Government in Pennsylvania, in Columbia Studies
in History, Economics, and Public Law, vol. 6 (New York, 1896), says Penn offered to add
a greater part of the territory for the £20,000. Penn himself says (B. of T. Papers, Props.,
P. 8; Q. 4) that he only offered the right of government. The case between Penn and the
Fords is discussed at length in Clarendon MSS. (Bodleian Library, Oxford), 102: 160.

[d] B. of T. Papers, Props., P. 27.

should be effected by act of Parliament, if not otherwise;[a] Quary represented to the Board that the province was in great confusion.[b] Penn therefore made a fourth effort (1710) to secure a price for the governmental powers. He asked the same amount as before, £20,000, but this was finally reduced to £12,000, payable in four years. Penn represented that the country had already come to maturity and was able to defray all the charges of government; that as a royal province the trade would increase and the customs, already amounting to £10,000 to £12,000 per annum, would become rapidly greater; that he had already paid out for settling about £50,000;[c] that the assembly was inclined to settle a revenue, and that the Queen's income from fines and forfeitures and from a duty on tobacco would be nearly £1,000 per annum. On February 2, 1711, Penn submitted some additional considerations on the terms of surrender. They are interesting in showing his motive and the constant difficulty he had experienced in maintaining his proprietary government because of "the easy ear the ministry from time to time lent to the unjust complaints of some designing and prejudiced men." In less than two years after his first going over he was obliged to return in its defense; and, when, in 1699, he had taken over himself and family to remain in the province, he was obliged to return very hastily to save his government from being wrenched out of his hands.[d] All the troubles since then were known to the Board and made him desirous in his declining years to deliver up the government into the hands that, as had so often been alleged, were most proper for it.[e] On consultation with Penn the Board decided to recommend the acceptance of the surrender, with the special proviso that the Quakers were to be under the Queen's protection.[f] Penn was paid £1,000 as the first installment of the £12,000 agreed upon;[g] but before the conveyances were completed and signed, Penn was seized with apoplexy and the agreements were never concluded.[h] An at-

---

[a] Penn-Logan Correspondence, in Pennsylvania Historical Society, Memoirs, vol. x, 196.

[b] B. of T. Papers, Pl. Genl. K, 1.

[c] Ibid., Journal O, 191.

[d] This reference is to the bill of 1701. See chap. iv post.

[e] B. of T. Papers, Props. Q. 9.

[f] Ibid., Q. 54; Entry E. 255.

[g] Calendar of Treasury Papers, cxliv, 31.

[h] Ibid., ccxxviii, 18.

tempt was made to carry the matter through by an act of Parliament, but it was defeated by the heirs at law. [a] Penn had devised the government of Pennsylvania in trust to two earls in order to complete the surrender in case of his decease. A friendly suit, brought in chancery to settle the claims of government, [b] dragged on so many years that the execution of the surrender was impossible. [c] When a decision, apparently in favor of the heirs, was finally reached, they had changed their minds in regard to the advisability of a surrender. And so the matter was dropped.

The proprietor's persistent enemies were not slow in finding the defect in his title to the three lower counties on the Delaware. Randolph (1701) presented to the board the three papers on which Penn claimed the government of these counties: the indenture of the Duke of York (August 24, 1682), the conveyance of Newcastle of the same date, and the act of assembly held at Uplands (September 6, 1682), by which the inhabitants desired to be governed by the same laws as those of Pennsylvania. [d] Whereupon the board took up the matter and consulted the attorney-general. Meanwhile, Quary hoping that the dissatisfaction caused by the troubles of 1701 between the representatives of the two colonies would stimulate them to sign, was endeavoring to secure petitions from the people of Delaware praying to be taken under the Crown. In this he was not very successful, the few churchmen alone supporting his wishes. [e] Penn was finally summoned to make his defense, which he did in the following terms: [f] " My title to the lower counties is by Deeds of feefement from the Duke of York and his letter of Attorney to his President and Surveyor General and Clark of the Peace to give me possession and submission, wch they readily did by Turf and Twig and Water; as also by a ready acknowledgement of me as Govern[r] in open Court of Sessions; and which (as covenanted to do in said deed) he intended a Confirmation and further grant by Letters Patent when king as appears by Sir Wm.

a B. of T. Papers, Props., Entry F, 418.

b Ibid., Props., Q. 181, 207; Calendar of Treasury Papers, cclv, 10.

c B. of T. Papers, Props., Q. 181, Entry G; 217.

d Ibid., Props., F, 71, 72, 73.

e B. of T. Papers, Props., I, 1, 2, 14.

f Ibid., Props., L, 3.

Williamses draught by his Order in 88 but Obstructed by ye disorder the Court was in a little before the Revolution."[a] This statement of the title not being satisfactory to the board, they represented to the Queen that Penn's lieutenant-governor should not be confirmed unless he signed an article by which the Crown reserved the right to resume the government of the lower counties.   Penn protested in vain, and his entire charter being in danger, he concluded that it was wise to sign the reservation.   Subsequent protests were also unavailing, and it grew to be the habitual requirement on the confirmation of every lieutenant-governor of Pennsylvania and Delaware that a reserve to the Crown of the right of government for the latter should be agreed to by the proprietor.   Thus the right of Penn to these lower counties was never legally recognized. Probably only their insignificance caused them to remain a part of his proprietorship.

An attempt was made in 1716 by the Earl of Sutherland to wrest the Delaware counties from the Penns.[b]   The board of trade recommended a suit in courts therefor, but the courtier favorite did not consider the game worth the candle unless he could acquire the province by the King's prerogative.

The failure of the attempt to establish royal government in Pennsylvania left this vast province to develop, under proprietary forms, a democracy almost as complete as that maintained in the corporation colonies of Connecticut and Rhode Island.   This result was not attained, however, without friction with the governors and conflict with the business interests of the owners of the estate of Pennsylvania.   The celebrated case of the taxation of proprietary estates, which reached so acrimonious a stage in the French and Indian war, shows how the political and economic interests of a proprietary colony acted and reacted upon one another.[c]   The board of trade took the position, before that unusual, of supporting the proprietors against the agents of the colony, and the clamor for the assumption of the government by the Crown quickly subsided.

---

a This is interesting as the only proprietary grant authorized by James II as King.

b B. of T. Papers, Props., Q, 110, 114, 134, 135.

c For complete discussion see Shepherd, History of Pennsylvania under the Proprietary Government, Chap. X.

THE CAROLINAS.

The Carolina proprietors were not bound to their settlers by ties of a common faith, as in Pennsylvania and the Jerseys, or by a precedent of good government, as in Maryland. They were great English noblemen, whose sole interest in the province was the profit it might afford them, whose ideal of government was a fantastic scheme of reproducing a feudal aristocracy on a vague and impracticable basis. The colony developed but slowly, the profits were small and uncertain, the colonists proved stubborn, and the ways of the wilderness unsuited to idealistic constitutions. The lords proprietors interested themselves but little in the management of the colonies. They left affairs in the hands of some secretary or agent, who was usually controlled by some of the shrewder dignitaries in the colonies themselves. The relations, therefore, of the colonists and the proprietors tended constantly toward opposition, and it was by the action of the people of South Carolina that the government was wrested from the proprietors' hands and vested in those of the King. The people of North Carolina, scattered and few, disregarded the instructions of the board of proprietors, defied their governors, and lived in a state of unrest and individual freedom bordering on anarchy. But the South Carolina colonists were more compact, more skilled in political management, and more capable of uniting for a common purpose. From them came the initiative that finally overthrew the proprietors' government.

The charter of Carolina had been in danger of revocation several times simply because it was of the proprietary type. It was included in the bills of 1701 and 1706, and the confusion in Carolina was the chief cause of the bill of 1715. The church acts of 1703 were not only repealed in 1706, but in the course of the complaints concerning them by the colonists' agents the charter was brought into danger, and by order of the Queen on an address of the House of Lords, the attorney-general and the solicitor-general were ordered to proceed by "quo warranto" against it on the ground that a part of the proprietors had approved of acts that were "contrary to reason and repugnant to the laws of England." [a]   But a question hav-

---

a B. of T. Papers, Props., O, 51, 60, 64, 65, 76; Entry E, 360, 382.

ing arisen of the privilege of a peer in Parliament, the matter was dropped in the privy council.[a]

After the failure of the bill of 1715, the agents of the colonists remained in England and constantly attempted to bring to the notice of the King and of the board of trade the distressed state of the province, and to have the Government taken from the proprietors.   On June 22, 1716, they submitted two memorials to the board, showing the value of the province to the Crown, its defenseless condition, the desertion of its inhabitants, and that the lords' proprietors were unable or unwilling to furnish aid.[b]   At the same time they presented similar appeals to the King in council, replying to the defense of the proprietors "in a very damaging fashion."[c] The board summoned the agents to a conference and requested a statement from the proprietors.   Meanwhile the agents had written to the colonists to continue their petitions and memorials, and early in 1717 a fresh batch arrived, signed by merchants, by the assembly, and by various groups of inhabitants.[d] A printed document was also prepared for both houses of Parliament.[e]   The agents had a hearing before the board (May 10, 1717), and after showing the deplorable condition of the province according to advices lately received, they declared that Lord Cartaret, the palatine, had told them he was willing to resign his share of the proprietorship if it would conduce to the relief of the colony.[f]   The proprietors in reply to the board's question declared that they had laid out several hundred pounds since the war began, and had given orders that all arrears of quitrents should be used for public purposes.[g] Lord Cartaret denied that he had offered to resign his proprietorship, and requested the board to suspend judgment until the new governor, Col. Robert Johnson, should arrive and report the state of affairs in the colony.   This reasonable request appears to have been granted.

[a] See McCrady, History of South Carolina under the Proprietary Government (New York, 1897), I, 427–438; a correct and complete account of this first attempt to void the charter.

[b] B. of T. Papers, Props. Q, 76, 77.   Printed in part in N. C. Recs., II, 229–233.

[c] Ibid, Q, 66, 79.   The agents hinted that there were Stuart intriguers among the appointees of the proprietors in South Carolina.

[d] One of these is from the French immigrants in their native language.   B. of T. Papers, Props. Q, 111, 116.

[e] Ibid, 117.

[f] B. of T. Papers, Journal S., 250, 251.   N. C. Recs., II, 280.

[g] B. of T. Papers, Props. Q, 121.

Meanwhile, the deed of surrender executed October 28, 1717, by the Bahama proprietors, who were nearly the same as those owning Carolina, encouraged the colonists' agents to press their interests.   In March, 1718, they renewed their representations of the dangers of the colony from pirates and Spaniards as well as Indians, and submitted a memorial signed by 568 persons, more than half of the male inhabitants of South Carolina, praying to be taken under the crown.[a]   But while the board of trade with their dilatory action were still questioning and inquiring, the impatient South Carolinians refused to remain longer under a government so inefficacious and so underhanded as that of the proprietors.   While ostensibly governing through their lieutenant-governor, the proprietors were in reality wholly influenced in their policy by Nicholas Trott, the learned but corrupt chief justice of the province, and by his unscrupulous colleague, Colonel Rhett. Acting upon their advice the proprietors had sent over a veto of several laws that the colonists considered essential to their welfare and liberty.   Upon the governor's proclamation of dissolution the assembly voted itself a convention of the people, seized the government into its own hands and elected a governor, confidently appealing to the English Government for support.   The good and loyal governor, Colonel Johnson, although he sympathized with the grievances of the people, could not do otherwise than attempt to suppress the rebellion against the proprietors.   But having no support he was obliged to yield.   The surprising news reached England early in 1720, and simultaneously the colonists' cause was strengthened by the arrival of their agent, John Barnwell, with explanations and addresses.   The revolutionists rested their cause on the charter, claiming that the proprietors had violated it in many particulars: they were to propagate the gospel and to transport a colony, but had done neither; they had hindered the people by violating covenants with those who had been induced to immigrate; good government and safety were a design in granting the charter, neither of which had been secured.   They also recited the recommendation of 1706 and then passed to the immediate troubles, the repeal of beneficial

---

a B. of T. Papers, Props., 151.

laws and the multiplication of negatives, the veto right being maintained by both governor and palatine.[a]

The English Government was only too willing to take advantage of the situation, even at the cost of encouraging the dangerous precedent of a revolution. The palatine, Lord Cartaret, being absent on a diplomatic mission, Mr. Ashley and Mr. Dawson attended several times on the board and at the privy council. In one of these conferences they admitted that they were in treaty for the sale of the province.[b] This still further enraged the people of South Carolina,[c] and rendered the English administrators more ready to supersede them. On August 11, 1720, therefore, an order in council was passed to assume the provisional government of the province, and September 20 a draft of a commission was ordered for Francis Nicholson as royal governor.[d] A hearing having been had by the proprietors, a third order was issued September 27, for the attorney-general to bring a "scire facias" against the charter.[e] This was, however, never done, and the royal government was merely a provisional one and the charter still in legal force.

In regard to North Carolina, the colonists' agents advised the resumption of that government also, since there was but one charter for the whole, suggesting that it might be better to annex it to Virginia, as nearer and more related thereto.[f] Nothing was done, however, and the proprietors continued for ten years longer to appoint governors for North Carolina.

Just before the arrival of the new royal governor in the colony, the proprietors' governor, Colonel Johnson, taking advantage of the presence of two men-of-war, whose captains agreed to support him, made an effort to recover the government for his principals.[g] The revolutionary government trained their guns upon the marines and brought the matter to an effectual stop. One of the captains acted as mediator,

a "True State of Case between the Inhabitants of South Carolina and the Lords Proprietors," B. of T. Papers, Props. Q., 203.

b B. of T. Papers, Journal W, 270-274. See McCrady, History of South Carolina, I, 668-670, for connection with South Sea bubble.

c B. of T. Papers, South Carolina, A, 18.

d Ibid, 1, 21, 22, 23.

e Ibid, 24.

f B. of T. Papers, Journal W, 503; South Carolina, A, 17.

g May 11, 1721. B. of T. Papers, South Carolina, A, 30.

the affair came to an end without bloodshed, and the proprietors' government in the colony of South Carolina was wholly destroyed. Their title, however, was still valid. After several ineffectual efforts to get this recognized, they offered to surrender their right to the government and all their interests in the Carolinas for £25,000.[a] This purchase was facilitated by the troubles in North Carolina with the proprietors' governor, who was not only a petty tyrant but a Jacobite as well.[b] An act accordingly passed both houses of Parliament and was signed July 25, 1729, accepting the surrender of the proprietary rights of seven of the proprietors. Lord Cartaret refused to join with the others and reserved his one-eighth share.[c] Some months after he petitioned to have his share set aside in one portion, offering to surrender his share of government for that privilege.[d] This was not finally consummated until 1744.

Thus this largest and latest of the proprietary governments to revert to the Crown was destroyed by popular action and revolutionary methods. It might have been a warning to the English Government that such colonists were as little likely to endure oppressive measures from the Crown as from the proprietors, and that the descendants of those who cited the breaches of the charter of 1663 in 1719 would cite Magna Charta in 1776.

THE BAHAMAS.

The case of the Bahamas was a simple one. In the track of the French and Spanish vessels, they were open to devastation in every war. The patent granted the proprietors in 1670 was not utilized with any efficiency for twenty years. A few settlers having gone out at the instigation of some merchants, a form of "squatter sovereignty" was proclaimed, and the inhabitants chose a Presbyterian preacher for governor in 1687 and fixed a capital at Providence. In 1690 the proprietors sent a governor whom the inhabitants refused to recognize. They imprisoned him and chose a president of their own. Again, in 1694, a governor was commissioned by the proprietors, but he was accused of sheltering pirates and

---

a House of Commons Journal, XXI.   May 24, 1728; April 9, 1729.

b B. of T. Papers, Props., R, 98, 99, 101–103, 106, 107.   N. C. Col. Recs., II and III.

c Rolls of Parliament, 2 George III, 7.   The price finally paid was £22,500.

d Additional MSS., British Museum, 32693, f. 37.

wrecking ships, and was imprisoned on his return to England. The inhabitants would have no proprietary governor. They drove out another in 1699 and sent a third to England in irons in 1701.   At last Nemesis overtook them in the shape of the Spaniard, who during Queen Anne's war twice plundered the islands and left them desolate.[a]   The proprietors thereupon abandoned all attempts to govern or defend them.   Gradually a few settlers accumulated on the islands and again chose their own governor, one Capt. Thomas Walker, who seems to have been a vigorous administrator.[b]   Several attempts were made to induce the English Government to fortify these islands and to vacate the charter.   In 1706 an order in council was issued to prosecute the case in the courts by a "quo warranto." This was stopped, like that against Carolina, by the privilege of peers in Parliament.[c]   Again, in 1709 and 1710, the Queen was urged to appoint a governor on the ground of an "extraordinary exigency," but nothing came of it.   In 1717, Capt. Woodes Rogers proposed to the proprietors to form a company to resettle the islands, on condition that their rights and privileges should be vested in the company for twenty-one years.   The property being absolutely worthless as it then lay, the proprietors inclined to grant this power to Captain Rogers, who promised them something of an income at the end of seven years.[d]   On inquiring the state of the islands it was learned that they had become a nest of pirates, no less than seven or eight hundred inhabiting Providence alone.   To rout and dispossess them required a considerable naval force, so it was decided to apply to the King for a royal commission and a sufficient force to support the enterprise.   This was accordingly done, and the proprietors executed a deed of surrender of all civil and military powers on condition that the government should remain distinct and not be annexed to any other, and that liberty and freedom of religion should be preserved.[e]   Thus the last of the island proprietary governments was extinguished.

---

a B. of T. Papers, Props., Q, 128.

b Ibid., Props., P, 99.

c Ibid., Props., P, 37.

d They were to have £100 per annum for the second seven years, and £200 for the last seven years. B. of T. Papers, Props., Q, 128.

e Ibid., 133. No money consideration being involved an act of Parliament was considered unnecessary, the acceptation of the proprietors' surrender vesting the government in the Crown.

CHAPTER III

ATTEMPTS AT INTERNAL CONTROL.

THE EXECUTIVE—THE JUDICIARY—APPEALS—THE LEGISLATURE.

It was the aim of the English administrators in their new zeal for colonial government not merely to bring colonies directly under the control of the Crown, but also to secure the largest possible measure of control in the colonies indirectly administered, because removed from their care by the intervention of a charter. Such control they attempted to secure in three ways: First, by enlarging their relations with the executive; second, by arranging a system of intercolonial courts; third, by continuing a check upon colonial legislation.

THE EXECUTIVE.

In the English colonial policy the governor was the connecting link between the English administrators and the colonial local government. In the colony he represented the dignity and majesty of the monarch himself. He commanded the militia; he presided over the supreme colonial court; he summoned, prorogued, and dissolved the assemblies; he held a power of veto; he was the source of pardons and of appointments to positions of trust and honor. Moreover, he was chief land agent, he held the power of making grants and of collecting quitrents. Thus the colonists' sentiments toward him were complicated by the two sets of relations—political and economic. From the standpoint of the home Government the governor was the royal agent. His appointment was for a term dependent upon the King's will. He was the means of communication between Crown and colony, the enforcer of the commercial system, the defender of the Crown's prerogative, the commander in chief in time of war. The difficulty, however, of efficient control over a governor at so great a distance was recognized by the home Government. A state paper of 1714 sets this forth.[a] The tendency, therefore, was

---

[a] A scheme or treatise of 1714, in B. of T. Papers, Pl. Genl. K., 39. "Governments have been given as a reward for services and with the design that such persons should make their fortunes. They are generally obtained by the favour of great men to some of their Dependants or Relations, and they have been sometimes given to persons who were obliged to divide the profit of them with those by whose means they were procured. The Qualifications of such persons for Government being seldom considered * * *. A bad

to reduce the governor's authority by means of a royal council and to appoint councilors directly without consultation with the governor.   His veto power was lessened by the consistent and constant efforts to have all legislation ratified in England, and his judicial authority was abridged by the drawing over of appeals to the English courts.

The colonists also sought to interpose their check upon the colonial governor by the control of his salary.   Except in Virginia, where the salary was paid by the Crown, a long succession of undignified bickerings on that subject marks the constitutional development of the American colonies.   This occurred also in the proprietaries and in Massachusetts.   The only colonies where harmony with the executive prevailed were the two corporations of Rhode Island and Connecticut, whose governors were simply executors of the legislature. But in all the colonies under the control of the charters, with the exception of Massachusetts, whose governor was of royal appointment, the colonial administrators lacked an agent of their own creation.   As the commercial relations between the mother country and the colonies increased and the need of protecting the colonies from French attack grew more impera- tive, this lack was felt as a distinct disadvantage, and plans for gaining some measure of control over the governors appointed by proprietors or elected by corporate colonies were welcomed with alacrity and pushed as vigorously as might be consistent with chartered rights.[a]

The plan fathered by Edward Randolph was to include in the navigation act of 1696 a series of measures which would secure effective enforcement of the acts of trade and check the connivance of the proprietary governments at illegal com- merce.[b]   The first of these measures was the royal confirma- tion of governors.   It was embodied in the act in the follow- ing language: ''And all governours nominated and appointed

---

Governor grows haughty and insolent, and there is great Difficulty of redress, if they prove all against him, the worse thing that can happen is his recall, after two or three years, when the usual term of such Governments is almost expired.   And he may enjoy at quiet in Brittain the fruits of all his oppression and rapine.''

[a] See letter of Canning, custom-house officer in Boston, March 2, 1717: '' But the charter governments are all enemies to the prerogative, and it would be a service to the Crown were they all taken away.   *   *   *   Where any Governor must depend on the People he cannot exert himself with that courage for the Crown's service as he could if he had no dependence upon them.''

[b] The proprietaries were, no doubt, especially involved in illegal trade.

by any such Persons or Proprietors, who shall bee intituled to make such nomination shall bee allowed and approved by His Majesty His Heirs and Successors as aforesaid."[a]

The machinery for carrying this provision into operation was not easily arranged. The proprietors of the Bahamas were the first to request royal approval for their appointee, Nicholas Webb, January 28, 1697.[b] Penn, owing to his absence in America, failed to get his lieutenant-governor confirmed, a fact which his enemies used to his disadvantage. The privy council requesting of the board of trade the names of the proprietary governors that had not been confirmed, it was necessary to send to Randolph in America to procure such a list.[c] Upon receiving Randolph's reply, and observing that only the Bahamas' governor had received the required approbation, the board urged the attorney-general to reply to the question submitted November 9, 1699, "how the Proprietors in His Majesties Plantat^{ns} may be more effectually obliged to present the names of the respective Governors appt^d by them for his Maj^{ts} allowance or disallowance."[d] He responded January 2, 1701, that "the Proprietors of the Plantations could not be more effectually obliged to present the names of their Governors to his Matie for his Approbation but by Act of Parliament, which was then intended to be endeavored the last session, and to be provided for by some Clause in the Act for punishing Pirates, but was omitted, and therefore I humbly conceive it must be attempted this next Parliament to procure a Remedy by some act to be made for that purpose."[e] Accordingly, the board of trade reported to the House of Commons in relation to the bill of 1701 that this was one of the grievances that made the vacating of the charters a necessity.[f]

With the failure of this bill, and the inconveniences attached to the annual approbation of the elected governors in the colonies of Connecticut and Rhode Island, this provision of the law was allowed to lapse so far as these corporations

[a] Statutes of the Realm, 7th and 8th William III, chap. 22. For the other features of this plan see "The Judiciary," post.

[b] Privy Council Register, 1694–1697, 575.

[c] B. of T. Papers, Pl. Genl., Entry B, 113. Props., F, 41. Received from Randolph, November 6, 1700.

[d] Ibid., Props., Entry A, 405.

[e] B. of T. Papers, Props., F, 56.

[f] Ibid., Pl. Gen'l, Entry B, 445.

were concerned.   Penn secured the approval of his governor
in 1702, on condition of a reserve to the Crown for Delaware.[a]
In the Carolinas no governor was presented for confirmation
until 1711.[b]   This provision of the act of 1696 was gradually
enforced among the proprietaries, and gave such measure of
control as resulted from the board's inspection of the records
and fitness of the candidates presented.[c]

The second measure, closely allied to the first and necessary
in order to make the confirmation effective, was the requirement concerning oaths to support the laws of trade.   By the
act before cited they were to be taken by all governors of
proprietary colonies as well as by those under royal appointment.   The amount of security to be given varied according
to the extent and importance of the colonial trade.   By this
means the governors in the charter colonies were held as
strictly to enforce the navigation laws as those in the colonies
under royal control.

An effort was made to compel the proprietors to give bonds
and security for their deputy governors.[d]   This culminated
in an address to the King from the House of Lords, March
18, 1697,[e] complaining of the illegal practices in the "several
great tracts of land granted by Your Majesty's predecessors
where the governors are not immediately nominated by Your
Majesty," and demanding that the proprietors be held responsible by a legal bond.   The latter at once offered objections.

Jeremiah Bass, agent for the Jersey proprietors, wrote:
"I am very sorry their Lo[ps] insist so positively on security
for the Gov[rs] of Proprietary colonies, since I find the Proprietors grow more and more averse to compliance and think it
too great a hardship upon them."[f]   Penn wrote, February 12,
1698: "I think it hard Proprietaries should give security for
Deputys of the king's approbation; since to me it seems the
same thing.   For therefore we should be excused because the
king approves or disapproves our nomination.   If we may
absolutely appoint I think we could not well refuse to be security for their obedience to the Acts of Navigation.   How-

a See Chapter II, ante.
b B. of T. Papers, Props., Q, 16; Entry F, 313.
c Occasionally one nominated by the proprietors was rejected.
d B. of T. Papers, Journal A, 29.
e Ibid., Pl. Gen'l, A, 4, 58.
f B. of T. Papers, Props., Entry A, 99.

ever, if it be thought fitt yt security be given even for such
as the king approves of, I humbly offer to you that no Deputy
be approved of yt will not give the king security for his right
discharge of the place in reference to trade and the king's
Revenues; since a Proprietary, that may be both absent and
Innocent may be ruined by ye carelessness or corruption of a
deputy and yt the Security arrived at by the Lords in their
address to the King is equally answered by this."[a] The reasons for the proprietors' reluctance is well explained here.
The conditions in the colonies made it impracticable for them
to pledge their money to secure the acts of trade.[b] October
27, 1698, the board reported to the King that none of the proprietors or the charter governments had given the security
required by the address from the House of Lords.[c] Upon the
opinion of the attorney-general that he could not "find any
Law whereby the Proprietors of Plantations are obligded to
give Security for their Deputy Gov'rs,"[d] the attempt was
abandoned. In 1722 the board of trade threatened Rhode
Island and Connecticut with a forfeiture of letters patent if
they did not comply with the terms of this address,[e] and they
were obliged to give the bonds for their governors to Governor Shute.[f] Again, in 1734, the committee of the House
of Lords on the state of the plantations gave an opinion that
these colonies should require their governors to give these
oaths and securities, but this never seems to have been
enforced.[g]

The complicity of the governors[h] with pirates led to an
act " For the more effectual suppression of Piracy," by which
commissions were authorized to be sent out to the governors
in order to try captured pirates and condemn them to death.
During the course of discussion upon this bill in the House,
an amendment was offered and accepted to the following
intent:[i] " And be it enacted That if any of the Governors in

[a] B. of T. Papers, Props., 1697, 433.

[b] Randolph wrote about this time: "No notice there [in South Carolina] is taken of the
acts of trade."   B. of T. Papers, Pl. Gen'l, A, 11.

[c] Ibid., Pl. Gen'l, Entry A, 370.

[d] Ibid., Props., F, 9.

[e] B. of T. Papers, Pl. Gen'l, Entry E, 456.

[f] Rhode Island protested, but to no avail.   Ibid., Props., R, 44.

[g] House of Lords Journal, XXIV, 411.

[h] Fletcher was accused by Bellomont, who says, "I have proved his correspondence
with pirates."   Clarenden MSS. (Bodleian Library), 102; 21.

[i] House of Commons Journal, XIII, 307.

the Said Plantations [those under Grants or Charters from Crown], or any person or persons in authority there shall refuse to yield obedience to this act such refusal is hereby declared to be a Forfeiture of all and every such Charters granted for the Government or Propriety of such Plantation," which amendment was accepted and approved.[a]   During all the discussion of piracy and its suppressions the board made constant accusations in regard to the governors of proprietary and of charter governments.[b]   For example, December 9, 1697, the board represented to the King; "Upon consideration of the manifold mischiefs that have of late years been committed in East India and other remote places, and the favorable entertainment, protection and encouragement which it is notorious many have found in several of your Majesty's colonies and plantations in America (and more particularly in Proprieties and Charter governments)" etc.   As a remedy it was proposed to pass a stringent law in Parliament to punish the governors of all plantations, not excepting those under proprietary or charter governments for any malfeasance in office.   This was accordingly done with the provision that the cases were to be tried in the English courts.[c]

In addition to these attempts to control the appointment of governors and to impose restrictions upon them in regard to the acts of trade, an attempt was also made solely by the action of the perogative overruling chartered rights to foist a royal governor upon the corporation colonies of Rhode Island and Connecticut.   During the first French war, when an urgent need for the union of all the northern colonies under one head was felt,[d] an opinion was obtained from the attorney-general that governors might be appointed by the Crown in a charter colony in case of pressing danger or a grave exigency,[e] and the militia of these colonies was actually placed under the authority of neighboring royal governors.   In 1704, in the course of the attempts made by Cornbury and Dudley to get possession of the small corporation colonies, this old opinion was brought to light.   Induced by the complaints of these

---

[a] Statutes of the Realm, 11 and 12, William III, c. 7.
[b] B of T. Papers, Pl. Genl., Entry A, 219, 232, 245; Journal, B, 444.
[c] Statutes of the Realm, 11 and 12, William III, c. 12.
[d] See Chapter IV, post.
[e] B. of T. Papers, New England, Entry E, 358.

officials that Connecticut and Rhode Island refused their quotas for the war,[a] and that "they hate any one that owns subjection to the Queen,"[b] the board of trade recommended that Dudley should be commissioned gòvernor of Rhode Island.[c] The report of the attorney-general was a strong one in favor of the prerogative.   He not only concurred that in an extraordinary exigency and in case of the inability of the proprietor or corporation to defend the colony a governor might be constituted, but "that as to the civil government such Governor is not to alter any of the rules of property or proceedings in civil causes established pursuant to the Charters granted, whereby the proprietors of those colonies are incorporated; on perusal of which Charters, we do not find any clauses that can exclude your Majesty, (who has a right to govern all your subjects,) from naming a Governor on your Maj^{tys} behalf, for those colonies at all times."[d]

The agents of Rhode Island and Connecticut in alarm prayed for a hearing, which was finally granted February 12, 1705. Meanwhile Cornbury had sent over a manuscript copy of Bulkeley's "Will and Doom," in a hundred closely written pages, to prove that Connecticut had illegally resumed her charter after the Andros régime.   The board meeting on this occasion was very large, including the great officers of State and the prince consort, George of Denmark.   The agents prayed for time and that the charges should be proved on oath.   The whole matter now became merged in the bill of 1706.[e]   Dudley, hoping by that means to become the royal governor of Rhode Island, dropped his former plan, and the board never again attempted to assert the prerogative against these colonies to the extent of appointing a governor for them.

The net result, therefore, of all the efforts to control the executive in proprietary and corporation colonies amounted to this: The proprietors were compelled to obtain for their governors confirmation by the Crown, before securing which the governor entered a bond and took an oath to observe the acts of trade.   The proprietors themselves gave no bonds for

[a] B. of T. Papers, Props., Entry D, 479; New England, Entry E, 344,358; New England, O.30.

[b] Ibid., New York, W. 30.

[c] Ibid., Props., Entry D, 413.

[d] Ibid., Props., M. 47.   Chalmers, Opinions, pp. 67,68.   It is strange that more advantage was not taken of this legal opinion of the right to appoint a royal governor.

[e] See Chapter IV, post.

the conduct of their governors. Spasmodic attempts, with slight success, were made to impose the same bond and oath upon the governors in the charter colonies elected by the people. The governors in the corporation colonies were not only exempt from all regulation, except general instructions from the home government, but their names were not even known at the office of colonial government. Occasionally a proprietary governor undertook to overreach his principals by direct communication with the royal administrators, but as a rule they were content to act as agents in the colonies, relying on the proprietors to effect arrangements with the English authorities. All governors, however, were liable to prosecution in the English courts, but this was never put into practice, the removal of a governor being considered a sufficient punitory measure.

THE JUDICIARY.

The legal system in the American colonies was not transported full-grown from England, or carried on with regard for English precedents and in accordance with the practices of English courts. It was rather a popular system of law, resting upon the necessities and conditions of colonial life, and administered by the colonists themselves in accordance with their own ideas of justice and equity.[a] In the corporation colonies of the seventeenth century the opportunity for the growth of local custom, unaffected by dictation from the English authorities, was more complete than elsewere. Protected by the charters which gave powers of erecting courts and establishing judicatures, the colonists administered justice in a vigorous if somewhat rudimentary fashion, established their own forms of procedure, and refused appeal to the King's courts in England. When the English administrators began to investigate more fully the conditions of government in the colonies, and particularly the difficulties in enforcing the acts of trade, the deficiencies of the legal systems in the colonies, the glaring inaccuracies in the court processes, the ignorance of the judges and administrators of law cried aloud for reform. The constant complaints by the revenue officers of the impossibility of enforcing seizures in

---

[a] See Reinsch, English Common Law in the Early American Colonies, University of Wisconsin Bulletin, No. 31. (Madison, 1899.)

the colonial courts suggested the establishment of a series of Admiralty courts in all the colonies which should be used particularly in cases affecting breaches of the acts of trade. Up to this time the Admiralty system in the colonies had lain in the hands of the governors, who, with every commission under the great seal, received also a commission from the lord high admiral,[a] as vice-admiral for the plantations. The board of trade as late as 1696 informed the governor of Massachusetts that the governors as vice-admirals had sole power of Admiralty jurisdiction.[b]

In the colonies under charters, where the governor had no such commission, the proprietors claimed vice-admiralty powers under the clause granting them rights "over land and sea," and the corporations under that giving them right to choose judges. In the Massachusetts provincial charter the power of vice-admiralty was reserved to the Crown, as was the erection of Admiralty courts. Possibly this was indicative of an intention to erect colonial vice-admiralty courts under the supervision and control of the English authorities. The inclusion of such courts in the navigation act of 1696, with power to try seizures for illegal trading, appears to have been part of the plan of Randolph and the commissioners of customs.[c] Randolph had complained in 1695 "that the illegal trade of the plantations was supported and encouraged by the Generall partiality of Courts and Jurys (byassed by private Interest) in causes relating to the Crown,"[d] and his first thought seems to have been the creation of an equity court. Thus in October, 1695, he submitted a series of "Proposalls to the Commissioners of Customs to discourage illegal Trade," the first of which was that a court of exchequer be established in all the colonies, with judges and attorneys-general appointed by the Crown.[e] On his return to England, however, he concluded that courts of Admiralty could be better employed to subserve the interests of the customs officers. So, after the passage of the bill known as the "Scotch act," he took immediate steps leading to the establishment of such royal intercolonial courts. He

[a] Admiralty Books, 1689–1692, p. 110; a sample commission of this kind.
[b] B. of T. Papers, New England, Entry A, 110.
[c] For the other features of this plan see the Executive, ante.
[d] Ibid., Pl. Genl., IV, 79. Printed in Prince Society, Edward Randolph, II, 144.
[e] Ibid., Pl. Genl., A, 10–16.

made a presentment to the commissioners of customs that if their officers were appointed by the Admiralty in England such courts would conduce to the due execution of the acts of trade.[a] To the board of trade he narrated the partiality of judges and juries composed of men interested in indirect methods of trade, and said he had never carried one cause in all these courts, even when there was unquestioned right on his side.[b] He was thereupon requested to present a list of names of persons suitable for this commission, and the matter was at once recommended to the King in council for immediate action. [c]

In the privy council the question whether this would infringe rights of the proprietors, and the related question whether the King could erect such courts in charter colonies at once arose. The proprietors took alarm and petitioned to be heard, that they might "vindicate themselves and those concerned from Mr. Randolph's Calumnies."[d] But the attorney-general rendered his decision against them, declaring that upon perusal of the charters of Rhode Island, Connecticut, Pennsylvania, Carolina, the Bahama Islands, East and West Jersey, Newcastle, and the county of Delaware, he does not find anything that restrains His Majesty from erecting courts of Admiralty in those plantations.[e] The proprietors maintained that the King had vested them with powers by sea and land, and that they conceived the power of Admiralty was included. They offered to establish such courts themselves, and though they insisted on it as a right would receive it as a favor.[f] But their arguments were overborne, the appointment of the persons recommended by Randolph took place[g] and commissions were issued out of the Admiralty office to that effect.[h]

The success of this uniform judicial system for the trial of breaches of the acts of trade in the colonies by royal officers was less than its promoters expected. In the first place, the officers were paid only by fees, and these were so inconsider-

---

a For the other feature of this plan see Pl. Genl., A, 5.

b B. of T. Papers, Journal A, 25.

c Ibid., Pl. Genl., Entry A, 27; August 13, 1696.

d Ibid., Pl. Genl., Entry A, 3; Journal A, 260.

e Ibid., Journal A, 263.

f Ibid., Journal A, 279.

g Ibid., Pl. Genl., A, 8, 117.

h Admiralty Books, No. 3, 96.

able that really competent men did not wish to hold these positions, particularly since they were objects of especial dislike in their respective communities. [a]

The first officers appointed under this act were of the Randolph faction, and thus exceedingly distasteful to the colonists. Every effort was therefore made to obstruct them in the business of their courts. In Pennsylvania an act had been passed November 7, 1696, providing for trial of breaches of the acts of trade by the colonial courts with juries.[b] The newly appointed vice-admiralty judge, Robert Quary, met opposition in attempting to hold his court. The entire government, he wrote, was active in exposing to the people that this court is arbitrary and illegal. In open council David Lloyd (the popular leader) had declared "that all those that any wayes did aid or encourage ye setting by of a Court of Admiralty in their Governm't were greater enemies to ye Liberties & properties of ye people than those yt sett up Shipp Money in King Charles ye first time * * * and now they have in opposition to the King's authority sett up a Court of Admiralty of their owne."[c] This led to an investigation, and Penn was summoned before the board and the privy council and ordered to replace the governor (Markham) for this and other offenses, to remove David Lloyd from the council, and to pay all due obedience to the court of Admiralty and the custom-house officers. The next year the trouble broke out again. Penn, having acted as required, wrote from Philadelphia defending the people against Quary's charges and saying that "they came hither to have more & not less freedom than at home."[d] Quary accused Penn of truckling to the people in order to get an appropriation from the assembly.[e] He complained that Penn had encroached on the Admiralty jurisdiction by granting commissions to "water bailiffs;" and on the failure of the bill of 1701 that would have revoked Penn's charter, Quary followed up his attack by coming to England and accusing Penn there.

For three months a very acrimonious contest raged before

[a] A tract of 1720 in the British Museum says: "The Judges, Advocates, Registers, and Marshalls of Admiralty, who have nothing to depend upon but the Fees of the Court, and being altogether unqualified for such employments by promoting litigations, actions, and pronouncing unjust decrees, have brought our Trade under a very Sensible Decay."
[b] B. of T. Papers, Props., C. 26, No. 8.
[c] Ibid., Props., C., March 11, 1699.
[d] Ibid., Props., F. 26.
[e] Ibid., Props., F. 56.

the board of trade, charges and countercharges clustering around this matter of the Admiralty.   Penn declared that Quary was unacquainted with the civil law, and argued that the greatest merchant in the province should not be judge and surveyor of customs, because as such he was partial in his administration and used his office for his own profit.   He admitted that he had been friendly with Quary until he found out his transactions.[a]   In his own defense and that of his colony he set up the obscurity of the law of the seventh and eighth of William III.   Finally the matter was submitted to the attorney-general, that a determination might be had of the entire subject of the Admiralty courts and their jurisdiction.   The attorney-general, Northey, held that the Admiralty courts were not established by virtue of the act aforesaid, but that this supposed them already settled there; that the common practice had been to sue for forfeitures under that act in such courts, and that although the act was confused, yet he was of opinion that Parliament intended this court with others in the plantations; that the informer had the option to sue in this or other courts in the plantations; and, finally, that by the terms of his charter Penn had not only a right to appoint water bailiffs (which are virtually sheriffs), but also to institute Admiralty courts of his own, "the power to constitute judges being to determine all causes within that precinct which must be causes there and not on the High Seas of which Admiralty Courts have cognizance."[b]   In this and a subsequent opinion[c] Northey disclosed a real ground for colonial opposition to these courts, since their jurisdiction was greater than that of Admiralty courts in England, and cases vital to the colonists' interests were placed in the hands of judges without trial by jury.[d]   Penn continued his case by direct appeal to the secretary of state and to the president of the privy council, being assured that Quary had the ear of the board of trade.[e]   He succeeded in getting Quary temporarily removed, but in 1703 he was restored.

---

[a] B. of T. Papers, Props., K. 9.

[b] Ibid., Props., K. 24.   This first opinion is not given by Chalmers.

[c] Ibid., Props., K. 48.   Chalmers Opinions, pp. 499-502.

[d] B. of T. Papers, Props., K. 34.   Penn replied to the charge of the ignorance of his judges, "If our judges are ignorant, they judge by the verdict of juries and not out of their own heads."

[e] Ibid., Props., L. 51.   Quary wrote, "It is the General discourse of the Quakers that the Lords of Trade and Plantations are Mr. Penn's enemies, but that he vallues them not having a greater interest than all of them, and shall be able to carry out his designs in spite of them all."

The new system of courts was not more popular in the other proprietary colonies. In the Carolinas the effort to establish them was unsuccessful until about 1701, when the judge wrote complaining of popular opposition. A similar complaint came from the Bahamas.[a] Connecticut seems to have submitted after the protest of Winthrop. In 1701 Atwood wrote from New York: "The Governour and Council of Connecticut were for some hours of opinion that it interferes with their charter. * * * But I think I left them in a disposition to submit to that jurisdiction, yet one of their Council being a Deputy Collector at New London the present seat of their Government I expect not to hear from thence of any Seizures or informations."[b] The people of Massachusetts, although one of their clergy maintained apropos of this Admiralty court that "they were not bound in conscience to obey the laws of England, having no Representatives there of their own choosing,"[c] did not attempt to resist the erection of the court, but tried to secure a judge upon whose local patriotism they could rely. Randolph wrote that Maj. Waite Winthrop had been appointed instead of Mr. Nathaniel Byfield, "who is strict for ye Observacon of ye Acts of Trade."[d] The Massachusetts authorities, moreover, proceeded against the Admiralty courts in the same manner in which the English courts of record had resisted their encroachments a century before—by the use of legal weapons in the other courts. In 1719 the Admiralty advocate wrote from Massachusetts complaining that the provincial judges "make frequent and intolerable encroachments upon the jurisdiction of the Admiralty in so much that they have of late proceeded so far as to set at liberty & discharge persons imprisoned by decree of the Admiralty Courts for debts and penalties due to His Majesty and do set aside by pretended prohibitions all appeals to the High Court of Admiralty and do issue out writs for large sums of money against masters of ships & others who sue in the Vice-Admiralty Courts." The governor refused to give redress, considering that by his vice-admiral's commission he made up the entire court. A similar complaint was also adduced by Judge Menzies of the

a B. of T. Papers, Props., H, 5.
b Ibid., New England, Entry D, 197.   N. Y. Col. Docs., IV, 930.
c Ibid., New England, Entry D, 197.
d Prince Society, Edward Randolph, II, 157.

same province with particular instances of encroachments, and the suggestion that this example was affecting other plantations. This was echoed by the commissioners of Admiralty, who said that they had received like complaints from other colonies "insomuch that it appears there is little or no regard had to the authority and jurisdiction of the Admiralty abroad."

The board in the meanwhile consulted their legal adviser Mr. West, who delivered a very interesting and remarkable opinion. After laying down the principle that the "Common law of England is the Common law of the Plantations and all statutes in affirmation of the Common law passed in England antecedent to the settlement of any Colony are in force in that Colony unless there is some private Act to the contrary, Though no Statutes made since these settlements are there in force unless the colonies are particularly mentioned," he went on to defend the rights of the plantation courts to issue out prohibitions, since common law has always been jealous of the encroachments of civil law and prohibitions have been the remedy constantly applied. The jurisdiction of the vice-admiralty courts, moreover, was made no greater by the acts of trade than of the Admiralty at home; in fact, where any penalty was exacted or recovered they were expressly excluded, since the terms describing these courts were common-law terms, which excludes the Admiralty. Also in all prosecutions to be made in courts of record the Admiralty was expressly excluded—the colonial courts being as much courts of record as that of the King's Bench.[a] In consequence of this opinion the board refused to support the Admiralty officers, and the colonial courts had a principle of resistance that they were not slow to utilize.[b]

In the charter colony of Rhode Island the resistance to the establishment of the Admiralty courts took definite form and led to most important results. This colony doubtless had good reason to dread too close inquiry into her privateering commissions and the harboring of pirates and illegal traders. Therefore, when Jahleel Brenton arrived with commission for Peleg Sanford (one of the opposition party) as judge of the Admiralty and for Nathaniel Coddington as register, the

---

[a] B. of T. Papers, Pl. Genl., L, 50. June 20, 1720. Chalmers, Opinions, 515–521.

[b] Ibid., Props., R. 110–131; S, 2; Entry H, 12, 15, 47. A complaint was made in Pennsylvania (1730) of such encroachments.

Quaker governor, Walter Clark, got possession of these papers and refused to surrender them. He also worked upon the feelings of the legislature, then in session, by telling them that such commissions were an infringement of their charter rights and privileges and that if they assented to them he would take his leave and there would be no more elections according to charter.[a] Six months later the board recommended that a commission be dispatched to Lord Bellomont to make a complete inquiry of the irregularities of this colony.[b] When the news of this commission reached Rhode Island, the governor wrote a most submissive letter to the board, saying: "We take it as a most bountiful favor that we can have liberty to answer for ourselves to so considerable a person & we hope to clear ourselves."[c] But in a speech at a special meeting of the assembly August 21, 1699, called to consider their difficulties, the governor was less guarded in his remarks. "The aforesaid premises considered, I doe conclude it lys befor this Hon[rd] Assembly to make what preparations can be for the Maintaining and vindicating our Just rights and priviledges according to our Charter, and I will assure you there shall be nothing wanting on my part to the best of my Skill and ability to maintain the Same, and hope it will be all your Minds and resolutions so to doe, and I am of that opinion we had better like men spend the one halfe of our Estates to maintain our priviledges than that we with our Children should be brought into bondage and Slavery as I may say (for I conclude it will be but very little better) for if we did but feel or was sencible of one halfe of what the poor people of Some other Governm[ts] suffer I doe believe we should be more vigorous to prevent what is likely to come upon us."[d] This unlucky speech, not at all intended to be bruited abroad,[e] nearly brought about the calamity it was intended to divert. The result of the commission increased the board's suspicions of the charter colony of Rhode Island and aided in forwarding the bill of 1701.[f]

[a] B. of T. Papers., Props., Entry A, 201, 2031. Printed in R. I. Col. Recs., III, 339.

[b] Ibid., Props., Entry A, 1698. The accompanying instructions are in R. I. Col. Docs., III, 363–367.

[c] Ibid., Props., Entry B, 110.

[d] B. of T. Papers, Props., D, 34.

[e] Ibid., Props., D, 73. "It is not made publick [the speech], but by accident I came to the sight of it and got a copy." Brinley to Lord Bellamont.

[f] Ibid., New England, Entry E, 211. A law of Rhode Island erecting a separate Admiralty jurisdiction was repealed at this time by the Queen. See Chap. iv, post, on Rhode Island's attitude toward the veto.

The friction between the Admiralty and the provincial courts increased as the number of cases increased and would doubtless have been still greater had the jurisdiction of the Admiralty courts been more regularly and efficiently maintained. After the French and Indian war the Admiralty courts were greatly extended in their operations, and the agitation in connection with the Stamp Act was largely due to the fear of the extinction of trial by jury in civil as well as maritime cases.[a] One of the clauses of the Declaration of Independence was a complaint of these courts, and particularly of a recent case in North Carolina. Their erection and continuation in the chartered colonies was a direct assertion of the prerogative. Taken in connection with the attempt to control their executives, it is an indication of the board's deliberate policy of asserting authority within the bounds of chartered exclusiveness.

APPEALS.

Throughout the entire history of the development of institutions there is no more effective weapon in the hands of centralizing authority than the power of taking over appeals from inferior courts of judicature—that is, of rehearing and redetermining any case in which judgment has already been given by a lesser court. By means of this entering wedge the administrative organs act indirectly but powerfully upon the laws, customs, and local government of a dependency, and in a most vital way modify and mold the local institutions according to the will of the central agent. In the Crown-governed colonies of the American continent the right of appeal from the decisions of the King's agents was a measure of protection against any unjust or arbitrary action on their part and a check on the overshadowing power of the provincial governor. In the corporation colonies, on the other hand, where popular sovereignty found expression, there was a reversion to the older type of appeal from the magistrates to the assembly of the people. Thus in 1642 we find a decree of the Connecticut legislature that the supreme power of appeal shall rest in the general assembly.[b] Appeal in such case from the decision of the people's representatives to the Crown was an intrusion on popular sovereignty, and in the terms of colonial thought a violation of charter rights and privileges.

---

[a] Life and works of John Adams (Boston, 1851), III, p. 466.
[b] Col. Recs. of Conn., I, 118; see also Mass. Recs., II, 16.

In the proprietary colonies, while the intervention of the proprietor between the people on the one hand and the King on the other rendered the action more complicated, the principle is clear. The King's justice was more desirable than that of the proprietor or his governor, and any resistance to royal appeals would come from the proprietors rather than the people.[a] In the charters of Carolina, Bahama, Pennsylvania, and the second one for Massachusetts Bay, appeal was reserved to the Crown. In that of Rhode Island an appeal was to be taken in case of dispute with any other colony. An appeal from the Jerseys was taken in 1696.[b] In New Hampshire the people looked with suspicion on an appeal taken by the proprietor to the privy council in order to recover quit rents,[c] but on the Crown's decision in their favor their confidence in royal justice was enlarged.[d]

In the period when the reins of colonial control were being more tightly drawn for the benefit of the prerogative, appeals were regulated in differing ways. In the colonies under the immediate supervision of the Crown they were restricted (after 1684[e]) by the requirement of security for their prosecution, and by various instructions to the governors (ranging from 1679 on), limiting the amount of the cases to be appealed to a comparatively large sum.[f] These regulations, by throwing more judicial authority into the governor's hands, worked for the benefit of the richer colonists and against popular rights.[g]

In the corporation colonies, on the other hand, appeals were a means of administrative interference with the rights of the people. The attempt, therefore, to draw them over to England was strongly resisted, both before the revolution of 1688, by Massachusetts, and later by Rhode Island and Connecticut, the strongholds of democratic sentiment and popular sovereignty ideas. In Rhode Island the governor and company followed their usual method of concession in words and resistance in acts. In theory they were always ready to

---

a Maryland Archives, Council Proceedings, II, 134. "Appeals to his Royal Majesty into England are termed [by the proprietor] criminal and denied."

b Privy Council Register, 1694–1697, 585.

c Ibid, 1701–1704, Dec. 17, 1702; also B. of T. Papers, New England, Entry C, 394, 399.

d Rawlinson MSS. (Bodleian Library), A, 379, 20, 22, letter of 1706 to Constantine Phipps.

e Additional MSS. (British Museum), 30372.

f Ibid. Usually about £300 was the sum required for an appeal in a civil case.

g In 1746 appeals were defined by a statute.

admit the King's prerogative and appeared mildly submissive before the constituted authorities; in practice they trusted to their insignificance to conduct matters as they chose. Thus (1699) Francis Brinley petitioned the King in council for redress on the refusal of the Rhode Island government to permit him an appeal. The board recommended that the governor and company of that colony be admonished to allow an appeal and that "further all persons whatsoever who may think themselves aggrieved by sentences given in the Courts be likewise allowed to appeal to your Majesty in Council."[a] To this the Rhode Island governor responded "wee do ashure yo[r] Lordships there was niver any appeale desired by sd Brinley of this Government much more a deniall, nither was there any other Person to our knowledge ever denied an appeale to his Majesty we haveing always held it as our Duty to Grant and his Majesties Right to Receive appeals from his agreved Subjects."[b]

The colony of Connecticut, therefore, was left alone to support the right of popular justice administered under the charter without recourse to the King. A case arose under a will devising certain lands to the ministry in New London, and the plaintiffs petitioned the King for an appeal without having submitted the case to the general assembly, evidently because, according to the statutes of that body, such an appeal would be useless. They grounded their petition on the violation of the statute of mortmain,[c] or on the contention that, there being no establishment of the Church of England in the colony, there was no "ministry" to whom the property could be devised. The board of trade, after considering the petitions, recommended that these cases and any others that may hereafter happen upon any difference between man and man about private rights be fairly judged in the colonies, and that any that think themselves aggrieved should have right of appeal, "it being the inherent right of your Majesty to receive and determine appeals from all your Majesty's Subjects in America."[d] This opinion was confirmed and sent to Con-

---

[a] B. of T. Papers, Props., Entry A, 411.

[b] Ibid., Props., D. 9. Newport, July 21, 1699.

[c] 6th Mass. Hist. Colls., III, 82. Winthrop wrote: "I am sure the foreign plantations are not named in statutes of mortmain, but our lawyers must say something for their fees."

[d] B. of T. Papers, Props., Entry A, 255.

necticut with a statement that "you are further to take notice
that he expects your speedy and punctual obedience thereunto
as you will answer to the Contrary."[a]

In October of the same year the general assembly of the
colony requested the governor and council to draw up a reply,[b]
which, couched in the dignified, courtly language of Winthrop, expresses the colony's resistance in the most careful
yet certain of terms.[c] The case under consideration is first
rehearsed in some detail, and then the report continues:

> As for the liberty of appealing from his Majesties Courts erected in this
> Colony To his Majesty in Councill, which is mentioned in your Lordship's
> Representation and his Majestie's order, Wee hope that since the com-
> plaints occasioning his Majesties declaring his pleasure therein were so
> groundless, wee shall not need to offer any further consideration there-
> upon. Wee could not possibly be more happy than to have all such
> differences as arise among us and not issuable here, to be heard and deter-
> mined by his Majesties great wisdome and Justice, did not the remote-
> ness of this Colony render it very prejudicial and almost wholly ruinous
> to his Majesties subjects here, to transport themselves over the vast ocian,
> and to be at that unavoidable charge; which the carrying and answering
> such appeals would oblige them to. We are therefore humbly bold to
> offer to your Lordships' thoughts his Majesties most gracious privilege
> granted by Charter to this Corporation for the hearing and issuing any
> such differences when they should happen among us. A power which
> because of the remoteness of this colony from his Majesties Kingdom of
> England (as is expressly said in the Charter) was thought necessary for
> the support of the same.

This address was not received or was mislaid, since it
was not read until December 5, 1700. Meanwhile a new
demand of the petitioner called out a sharp letter from the
board to the colony, saying, "We are not a little surprised
to have received no answer. * * * This long delay gives
us just reason to doubt your having rendered that prompt
obedience that was expected of you."[d] The board's annoyance was aggravated by the continued petitioning of the
appellants, who accused the governor of having said publicly
that no appeals should be allowed from there, and that they
would dispute the point with His Majesty.[e] Matters began

---

a B. of T. Papers, Props., Entry A, 409.

a B. of T. Papers, Props., Entry A, 409.

b Conn. Col. Recs., 1689–1705, 300.

c B. of T. Papers, Props., Entry B, 353.

d Ibid., Props., Entry B, 214.

e Ibid., Props., Entry B, 391. Winthrop is reported to have said: "We will grant no
appeals to England, but will dispute it with the king, for, if we should allow such
appeals, I would not give a farthing for our charter." (See Props., O, 23.)

to look serious for the colony, especially as this affair of the appeal became involved with other charges leading up to the bill for revoking all charter privileges.

In a report to the House of Commons April 23, 1701, one of the most effective charges made against Connecticut was not only that the colony had refused an appeal, but that the governor had made a rebellious declaration.[a] The attorney-general and solicitor-general, when consulted, affirmed the board's opinion that to hear appeals was a right inherent in the Crown.[b] Thereupon the colony of Connecticut thought wise to instruct its agent to memorialize the board and present the colony's position in as favorable a light as possible.[c] The grounds of the colony's opposition and the arguments advanced show clearly the importance of the matter from the standpoint of the colony and the essential weakness of their position from the point of view of the English administrator. They argued that a final appeal to their general court was expedient and in no way injurious to the prerogative. Their reasons were these: First, the distance renders an appeal to England difficult, since the colonists are drawn to a remote and *foreign* jurisdiction;[d] the insistence upon it will hinder immigration, and there has been "no precedent for such an appeal from incorporation to this day." In the second place, a final appeal to their general court is agreeable to their charter, since the legislative power is vested in the company "and, sure, the executive power to put these laws in execution must follow." Thirdly, withholding of appeal is not without precedent, since in England there are lesser courts from which no appeal is allowed. To the objection that, without appeal to England, they will be independent of the Crown, the memorial replies that no such consequence could follow, for if the general assembly should become corrupt ("which is a thing scarce possible to be supposed") there would be forfeiture of the charter and the colony would be seized into the King's hands.

This remonstrance failed of effect, and June 12, 1701, the petition for appeal was admitted by the privy council on representation from the board of trade.[e] After a hearing and

a B. of T. Papers, Pl. Genl., Entry B, 446.
b Ibid., Props., G, 18.
c Ibid., Props., Entry B, 358. Printed in Hinman, Letters from the Kings, etc., 286.
d The italics are mine; the word indicates the habit of mind of Connecticut people.
e Privy Council Register, 1699–1701, 218.

consideration of the colony's address the judgment of the colonial court was maintained[a] and the appeal dismissed. But the principle of permitting appeals was strictly maintained and the colony called sharply to account for any refusal. [b] The Connecticut authorities, however, continued to evade the demand, and never admitted the principle that appeals could be drawn from their chartered limits.

In judicial matters, therefore, the interference of English authorities was successful. An intercolonial judiciary was erected, with officers appointed by the Crown, acting under admiralty law, and trying cases without juries. Cases of civil nature, vitally affecting the economic and personal interests of the colonies, were tried in these courts. The right to take appeals from all colonies, whether protected by charters or not, was asserted as a prerogative of the Crown, and was successfully maintained against all resistance.

THE LEGISLATURE.

The distinguishing feature of the American colonial government was the local legislature, which gave the colonists an organ of government for the expression of their own needs and purposes. The colonists resisted strongly the efforts of English administrators to interfere with their legislative action. They submitted reluctantly to the royal veto upon their laws. In consequence, English control of the legislative action of the colonies was of slow growth and was never entirely complete.

The early requirement of the charters, that "laws shall be consonant with reason and not repugnant to the laws of England," was discovered to be insufficient. But no permanent requirement that colonial laws be sent to England for confirmation or approval seems to have been made until after the Restoration. In 1662 the governor of the colony of Jamaica was instructed that the colonial laws would only be in force two years unless confirmed by the King.[c] The same year Governor Berkeley, of Virginia, wrote: "They will in future print their laws for their Lordships' approbation, amendment or rejection so that errours can not be of more than one year's duration."[d] When the government of

---

a Privy Council Register, 1701-5, 489.   c Cal. Col. St. Papers, II, 259.
b Ibid., 476.   d Ibid., July, 1662.

New Hampshire was taken over by the Crown in 1679 the royal commission to the president of the council contained this clause: Laws " shall stand and be in force until the pleasure of us, our heirs & successors shall be known, whether ye same laws & ordinances shall receive any change or confirmation or be totally disallowed & discharged."*a* Again, in 1682, the commission to Governor Cranfield contains the proviso that "all such laws, statutes and ordinances of what nature & kind soever be, within three months or sooner after the making of the same transmitted unto us under the public seal, for our allowance and approbation of them," the King to have the right to annul these acts at any subsequent time according to his pleasure.*b* This was incorporated into a general provision in 1684, and introduced into the commission of each royal governor thereafter appointed.*c* A large part of the colonial series of documents in the record office of England consists of these acts sent over for the royal approbation.

The case in the colonies under charters was different. Massachusetts Bay stoutly resisted any suggestion that her laws should be sent to England for inspection, and that was one of the charges that led to the forfeiture of her first charter. Pennsylvania's charter contained the requirement that all laws should be presented to the privy council within five years from their time of passage, and six months was allowed the Government to approve or disapprove.*d* By her second charter Massachusetts was required to send her laws to England, where, if not disallowed within three years, they became valid without further action. None of the other proprietaries or corporations was under obligations to present its laws for approval in England, and no such custom was a part of their habitual action. This omission the board of trade set itself

a New Hampshire Provincial Papers, I, 373.

b Ibid., I, 435.

c The same was incorporated into commission of Dougan as governor of New York, 1686 (N. Y. Col. Docs., III, 369, 377); in Nicholson's instructions for Virginia in 1698 (Virginia Magazine of History, II, 49), and in Copley's commission as royal governor of Maryland (Maryland Archives, VIII, 263).

d This provision was the cause of much complaint in the privy council, six months being deemed insufficient time for examining the laws. In 1709 the board made a representation that "it is unreasonable that Mr. Penn should have five years to lay his laws before Your Majesty, and Your Majesty but six months to consider thereof." (B. of T. Papers, Props., Entry F, 146.) Nothing was ever done about it. In 1705 out of 105 acts submitted 36 were repealed.

to remedy. In 1697 the secretary was ordered to write to the proprietors of East and West Jersey, Pennsylvania, the Carolinas, and Bahamas for the laws of each colony, and soon after letters were sent to Connecticut and Rhode Island requiring them to send copies of their laws to England.[a] The Carolina proprietors replied that they had sent to the colony for them.[b] Rhode Island adopted the theory that they were "wholy ruled and Govern'd by the Good and wholesome Laws of our mother the Kingdom of England as far as the constitution of our place will bear and we doubt not but your Lordships are sensible that in these Remote parts we cannot in every punctillo follow the niceties of the Laws of England, but it will be a great damage to his Majesties' interest in the settling & peopling the Country."[c] The governor of Connecticut, on the other hand, maintained the sovereignty of the local assembly in making laws "suitable to the constitution of affairs in this wilderness,"[d] and while courteously conforming with the demand of the board of trade that their laws should be sent for inspection and requesting a favorable opinion of them from their lordships, asserted that the only power that could modify or repeal these acts was the general assembly of Connecticut.[e] By no other colony was the legislative independence so consistently and persistently maintained as by Connecticut.

In 1705 the Quakers, instigated by Cornbury and Dudley, presented a petition to the Crown in opposition to an act of the Connecticut assembly against their mode of worship. An order in council was obtained repealing the law "as contrary to Liberty of Concience allowed by the laws of England to dissenters." The colony nullified the force of this blow by itself abrogating the law at the next meeting of the assembly.[f] But in 1728 a more serious difficulty arose over the intestacy law, and dragged along for many years.[g] The act was repealed by the privy council, but this decision was not accepted in Connecticut, and a reversal was finally obtained in 1745. The Connecticut authorities never admitted the validity of the repeal, stoutly maintaining that "it is the privilege of

a B. of T. Papers, Journal B, 373, 383.

b Ibid., Props., 1697, 443.

c Ibid., Props., Entry B, 59.

d In the code of 1702 the preamble asserts that the laws of England are not in force in Connecticut unless reenacted by the general assembly.

e B. of T. Papers, Props., 1697, 561.

f Talcott Papers, I, 143.

g See Andrews: "Intestacy law in Connecticut," Yale Review, 1894.

Englishmen and the natural right of all men who have not
forfeited it to be governed by laws made by their own consent."[a] The board of trade vainly attempted during this dispute to force an explanatory charter upon Connecticut, as
had been required in Massachusetts, saying that "the people
of Connecticut have hitherto affected so intire an Independency of the Crown of Great Brit[n] that they have not for many
years transmitted any of their Laws for his Majesty's Consideration, nor any accounts of their Public Transactions."[b]

The immunity of the charter and earlier proprietary gov
ernments from the necessity of submitting their laws for approval or disallowance in England was not only maintained in
America and permitted in England, but was affirmed by legal
authority. In 1714 the attorney-general reported that "As
to law made in proprietary plantations, I am of opinion, that
mischief cannot be remedied there but by an act of Parliament of Great Britain; for that the Proprietors thereof have
a right vested in them of the power of making laws granted
by their charters, and are not, nor can now, be put under any
other restraint or regulation than such as are contained in
their respective Charters but by act of parliament."[c] The
same was reaffirmed in 1732 in regard to Rhode Island, "no
provision being made for that purpose [in the charter] the
Crown hath no discretionary power of repealing Laws made
in this Province, but the validity thereof depends upon their
not being contrary but as near as may be agreeable to the
Laws of England regard being had to the nature and constitution of the Place and People. Where this condition is
observed the Law is binding."[d] In 1734 an attempt was
made to remedy this by parliamentary action. A committee
of the House of Lords reported their opinion that "all laws
made in the plantations as well those under Proprietary or
Charter Governors as in those whose Government is immediately vested in the Crown be for the future transmitted home
for His Majesty's consideration within twelve months after
passing and no law to have force without his Majesty's approbation except the laws necessary for defence in an emergency."[e] But no action was taken on this report.

---

[a] Talcott Papers, I, 158.

[b] B. of T. Papers, Props., Entry H, 24.

[c] Ibid., Props., Entry F, 418. Printed in Chalmers, Opinions, p. 339.

[d] B. of T. Papers, Props., R, 29.

[e] House of Lords Journals, xxiv, 411. This was during the investigations of colonial
bills of credit or paper-money issue.

The case of Pennsylvania was peculiar, and at first legislation seemed to labor under the disadvantage of a triple veto—that of the lieutenant-governor, of the proprietor, and of the Crown. The proprietor insisted on his own negative, but the dissatisfaction of the people compelled him to yield and to transfer his right to his deputy governor; and in 1705 the attorney-general gave an opinion that, having thus deputed the veto power to his deputy, he had no right to reserve any such power for himself.[a] The Crown veto was, however, active, and many Pennsylvania laws were repealed. Incident upon this confirmation of the laws, many disorders and abuses crept in. In 1749 three acts of Pennsylvania were repealed, dating back for twenty and twenty-five years, on the theory that they had been laid before the board of trade and not the privy council. The colony was much alarmed and felt that such a policy would subvert their entire code; but upon petition of the proprietors the affair was dropped.[b]

A practice also arose of purchasing the confirmation of much-desired laws by judicious bribes applied to the proper persons. The negligence of the colonial agents in submitting acts was complained of as early as 1724, when the board represented that the colonies were, many of them, governed by laws that had long been repealed by the Crown, arising from the carelessness of their agents, "who seldom give themselves the trouble of taking out any Order in Council either for the repeal or confirmation of Acts wherein private persons are not concerned."[c]

Another method of evasion was to pass a law for a brief period, expiring before assent or dissent in England could be obtained, and then reenacting it in the same fashion. In 1697 the board of trade observed the effects of this practice and drew up a representation on the subject, wherein they said that the laws, "if disallowed by His Majesty yet being reenacted may be in force contrary to the express declaration of His Majesty and his Supreme authority be eluded."[d] Accordingly, an instruction was ordered to be inserted among those of the royal governors that all laws should be made indefinite and without limitation of time, except those neces-

---

a B. of T. Papers, Props., N, 48.
b Colonial Records of Pennsylvania (Harrisburg, 1851), V, 590.
c B. of T. Papers, Pl. Genl., Entry F, 15.
d B. of T. Papers, Pl. Genl., Entry A, 176.

sary for some temporary end. This did not check the practice in Pennsylvania, for in 1714 the attorney-general, Edward Northey, gave it as his opinion that this mischief could not be remedied in the proprietary and charter plantations except by act of Parliament,[a] and the whole matter was urged as part of the necessity for the bill of 1715 forfeiting all charters. After the failure of that bill, the practice continued, and in 1719 the attorney-general again reported that there was nothing in the charter of Pennsylvania to prohibit the reenactment of the substance of any law disallowed by the Crown.[b] So by this means an effective method of nullifying the royal veto was in use in Pennsylvania, and furnished a model of evasion to the other colonies. In consequence, Parliament requested the King in 1740 to send an instruction to all the colonial governors that they should assent to no law that had not a clause suspending its action until it had been transmitted to England for consideration. Nothing came of this at the time, but in 1752 such an instruction was inserted among those of the royal governors.

In general, therefore, the attempt to control legislation by a veto was successful in the royal provinces, but failed of effect in all charter colonies, except where a veto had been expressly reserved to the Crown. The effect of the charters was to check the operation of the royal veto, to foster the idea of legislative independence, and to develop in the colonists that feeling of responsibility for their own government that weakened their reliance upon the English administrative agents and their allegiance to the Crown. Especially was this true of Connecticut, of which it was written in 1740: "This government is a sort of republic. They acknowledge the king of Great Britain for Sovereign, but are not accountable to the Crown for any acts of government, legislative or administrative."[c] The other colonies looked with a degree of envy upon Connecticut, Rhode Island, and Maryland because of immunity from revision of their laws; and the complaint in the Declaration of Independence of the Crown's disallowance of " laws the most necessary and wholesome for the public good " may be traced in part to this feeling.

---

a Ibid. Pl. Genl., K, 35.   Printed in Chalmer's Opinions, pp. 338–340.
b Ibid., Props., Q, 171.
c Additional MSS. (British Museum), 30372, fo. 53.

Chapter IV.

PARLIAMENTARY PROCEEDINGS AGAINST THE CHARTERS.

TENDENCIES TOWARD UNION—BILL OF 1701—INFLUENCE OF THE ENGLISH CHURCH—BILL OF 1706—ACT UPON FOREIGN COIN—BILL OF 1715— DEFENSE OF CHARTERS.

TENDENCIES TOWARD UNION.

One heritage of the revolution of 1688, fraught with vast consequences to the American colonies, was the commencement of the second hundred-years' war between France and England and the need that ensued of defense and military equipment. No account of eighteenth-century administration can omit considering that the colonists suddenly found themselves confronted by the Indians organized by their French antagonists and ready to fall on their border settlements and to capture and massacre their inhabitants. The French, though vastly inferior in numbers, were rendered formidable by their centralized system of government, which gave the direction of affairs into the hands of one supreme governor and military commander; and the English colonists were at a disadvantage because of their lack of unity in plan and operation and the local jealousies that separated the provinces. The exposed colonies of New York and Massachusetts (on her Maine frontier) expected support from their neighbors in Pennsylvania, the Jerseys, Connecticut, and Rhode Island, which was at all times given with reluctance.

The previous union of New York and all the New England colonies under Andros formed a precedent, and in 1690 the militia of Connecticut and Rhode Island were put under the orders of Sir William Phips. After his disastrous Canadian expedition, while Fletcher was endeavoring to protect the New York borders against retaliatory raids, the command of the Connecticut militia was transferred to him by a special commission issued in 1693.[a] The Connecticut authorities resisted this as

---

[a] N. Y. Col. Docs., IV, 29.

an invasion of their charter rights, and Fletcher's attempt to enforce his authority has become a tradition among Connecticut historians. They tell how he came to Hartford with his suite, ordered the militia drawn up to listen to the reading of the royal document, how Captain Wadsworth ordered his drummers to drown the sound of the reading by the roll of their drums.[a] The colony immediately drew up a petition to the King, signed by 2,182 persons, requesting a continuation of their charter privilege to command their own militia,[b] and appointed Winthrop their agent to go to England and present their appeal.

Fletcher wrote in surprise and annoyance:

"I have been in this Collony 20 dayes laboreing to perswade a stubborne people to theire dewty. * * * [They] Have sepperated not only from the Church, But Crowne of England, and allowe of noe appeale from theire Courts nor the Lawes of England to have any force amongst them, some of the wissest have saide wee are not permitted to vote for any members of Parliam[t] and therefore not lyable to theire lawes. * * * I never sawe the like people They have raised a considerable Tax to send one M[r]. Winthrop theire Agent for England yett pay noe obedienc to the Crowne nether theire Agent or any in office have taken the oathes or subscribed the Test. I could not force obedience haveing noe Company but a few servants and two freinds nor did I think it the King's service to carry on the contest to Bloude tho they threaten to draw mine for urging my Masters right."[c]

Meanwhile the Rhode Island government had protested in like fashion against Phip's commission to command their troops, and had sent over a petition by their agent, Christopher Almy, for confirmation of their charter, adjustment of the eastern boundary, and continued command of their militia.[d] The attorney-general reported in favor of the validity of their charter, but reserved his opinion on the commission to Phips.[e]

The report on the petition of Connecticut maintained "that their Majesties may constitute a Chief Commander who may have authority at all times to command such proportion of the forces of each colony as their Majesties shall think fit and further in time of Invasion and approach of the enemy with

---

[a] Trumbull, History of Connecticut (New Haven, 1818), I, 390-369.
[b] Conn. Col. Recs., III, 102; N. Y. Col. Docs., iv, 69.
[c] N. Y. Col. Docs., IV, 71.
[d] B. of T. Papers, New England, Entry 1692-95, 117; printed in R. I. Col. Recs., III, 294-297.
[e] B. of T. Papers, New England, Entry 1692-95, 126; printed in R. I. Col. Recs., III, 293.

the advice and assistance of the governor of the colonies to conduct and command the rest of the forces."[a]   Governor Fletcher, however, was instructed upon Winthrop's solicitation to refrain from asking more of Connecticut than a quota of 120 men.

Nevertheless a governor-general and commander in chief for all the northern colonies was strongly demanded by a large party in the colonies, composed of property owners and merchants—responsible men who felt the pressure of the French war and the need of more united action.   A memorial was offered February 1, 1697, of the "Inhabitants, Traders, Proprietors etc. in the North parts of America being under very deep apprehensions, and discouragements from the late attempt of the French in these parts where we have in a manner lost our Fishing, Furr, Mast Timber, and Peltry Trade both at Newfoundland, New England and New York," the consequence will be the subversion and overthrow of these countries.   This has emboldened us to ask that "some good form of Gov[t] may be established for uniting of so many interests as is occasioned from diverse separate Gov[ts] and to enable us for any attempt of the Enemy."   We think the thing not impossible—

but may be so established under one Governour as to preserve to each their Civill Rights Properties and Customs even as in England, where notwithstanding the diverse Corporations of severall Towns in most of the Shires, yet for uniting and strength of the whole his Majesty hath in each County a Lord Lieutenant who hath command of the Forces of said province &c.

Now whereas under Said Gov[ts] as they were joined from the year 1686 to 1689 great confusion did arise, the disorders whereof that then happened ought not to be attributed unto the Union of the Colonies but from the Exorbitant and Illegal Commissions then granted and the no lesse exorbitant manner of executing the same, the inconveniences may be prevented by the just and prudent measures which the Court may take in sending a person of worth and honour, whose power and Instructions may be under such regulations as may render his Gov[t] easy to all, honourable to his Majesty and of advantage unto his realme &c.   The Premises considered we humbly beseech your Lo[ps] to take speedy resolutions therein and to make such Report to his Majesty as that your Pet[rs] may have reliefe by joining all the several Gov[ts], Civill and military, under one head. [b]

This desire for union even went so far as to demand a single strong centralized government for all the northern provinces

[a] B. of T. Papers, Journal 7, 286.
[b] B. of T. Papers, New England, A, 53.   There are 31 signatures.

to take the place of the "numerous little petty governments;"[a]
but the Liberty party took exception to the desire for a civil
head and the obliteration of colony lines, citing the charters
as instruments that rendered this impossible, and the force of
the movement spent itself in arranging for a commander in
chief who should be civil governor of New Hampshire, Massachusetts, and New York and should have command of the
militia of Rhode Island and Connecticut and the Jerseys, in
time of war only.[b]

Mr. Edmund Harrison's memorial well explains the situation:

> The English colonies being planted at severall times and by distinct
> grants from the Crown having different interests in Trade, looke on them-
> selves as so many distinct Principalities, are jealous of each other, and
> stand upon their separate Laws & Customs to the prejudice and weakening
> of the whole, for though they may be fifteen or twenty to one of the
> French, yet being without a Head in so many small Bodies and separate
> Interests may be an easy conquest to a smaller united Party. * * *
> That therefore such advantagious settlements may not be either ruined or
> cutt off from England it's humbly proposed as of absolute necessity that the
> Person His Majesty shall be pleased to send Governour of New England
> may also be the Civill Governour of New York and New Hampshire and
> Generall of all the Forces of New England, New York, New Hampshire,
> Connecticut, Rhode Island and the Jerseys * * * that no breach be
> made on any of the Grants and Privileges of the several provinces in their
> Civil affairs. [c]

Even this careful guarding of rights and privileges was not
enough for the separatist interest of the several colonies. The
agents of New York at once protested that "New England can
not protect New York, nor New York New England," and that
the governor's residence would be in Boston, their rival in
trade, and so he would not be on hand for any sudden danger.[d]
Mr. Samuel Allen, of New Hampshire, protested for his colony that it had been a separate government since 1682, and
there was no more reason it should be submitted to Boston

---

[a] B. of T. Papers, Entry A, 156. Benjamin Davis, of Boston, writes to his correspondent
in London, Edward Hull: "Sir: We are in a sad posture for want of a settlement and
help from the King. * * * Our people are very sorry that the King continues so many
little petty governments with us, as Piscataqua and Rhode Island, which, if not altered,
will be a means to ruin this government."

[b] B. of T. Journal, A, 393. Sir Henry Ashurst and Mr. Edmund Harrison declared to
the board that they had, with several others, hastily signed the memorial for uniting the
governments under one civil and military head. They wished the word "civil" omitted,
which was accordingly arranged.

[c] B. of T. Papers, New England, A, 54.

[d] Ibid, A, 61.

than Pennsylvania, Carolina, New York, or Connecticut.[a] Winthrop presented a memorial against the project on behalf of his colony,[b] adding that if any " general commander should have power to draw out their forces contrary to the Rights of their Charter by which they have subsisted threescore years, it would be the absolute ruin of it."[c] Mr. Brenton, the agent for Rhode Island, while making a similar protest, said he believed that his colony would be willing to surrender its charter if suitably rewarded. [d]

The sentiment for union was very strong in view of the exigencies of the situation. An interesting letter from Capt. Stephen Sewall,[e] of Salem, Mass., dated November 2, 1696, declares that the people, worn out with watching against the French, are moving away to South Carolina and other southern colonies, and wishes His Majesty would reduce all the governments to three: New Hampshire, Massachusetts, Rhode Island, and Connecticut into one; New York, both Jerseys, and Pennsylvania into another; Maryland, Virginia, and the Carolinas into another;[f] and set a great nobleman and soldier over all the said governments "so that we might make one body and purse, and we sh'ld send all French and Indians a grazing quickly. If the king does not take pity, I do not know what will become of us. I propose this only for the pure good of all. I am a true Englishman and a loyal Williamite." This is also the time when William Penn proposed his " Briefe and Plaine Scheam" for a general Congress of the colonial representatives to "heare and Adjust all matters of Complaint or difference Betweene province & province," as intermigration, escape of fugitives from debt and justice, defense against common enemies, etc., with a commissioner appointed by the King as president of the Congress.[g]

The necessity for unity in military matters determined the board to represent to the King that "it is hardly possible the

---

a B. of T. Papers, Entry A, 121.

b Ibid., A, 125..

c B. of T. Papers, Journal A, 393.

d Ibid, 49. Brenton, however, belonged to the King's party, and spoke without authority from his principals. If he was correct in his statement it was the only time a corporation colony offered the surrender of its charter.

e B. of T. Papers, New England, A, 64.

f An early perception of sectional grouping.

g B. of T. Papers, Pl. Genl. A, 40. Printed in full in N. Y. Col. Docs. IV, p. 296, 297; also in Frothingham, Rise of the Republic of the United States (Boston, 1892), pp. 111, 112.

colonies can be preserved without some Captain General." They recommended that one governor be appointed for the three royal colonies, who should have power to command militia in the three colonies under charters in time of war, according to the right expressed in the opinion of the attorney-general in 1694. [a] Lord Bellomont was thereupon chosen as the most suitable person to carry out this plan. The smaller corporation colonies made no immediate protest because the peace of Ryswick had been signed before he arrived in America, and thus this part of his commission was suspended.

All these bickerings concerning the control of the militia and the difficulty of securing unity of action for war had called the attention of the board of trade to the undesirability of charter governments. In a representation to the King the board affirmed that all other union except under a military head is "at present impracticable." Apparently a purpose was being formed to sweep away the charters as an impediment to their plans, and this project was being strengthened by the complaints against the colonies under charters that poured in from every side. That grave irregularities flourished under cover of these charters could not be denied. Lord Bellomont, whose policy was one of conciliation and support of the popular party, was obliged to report the evils of the Rhode Island government. There is such a "bloody crew of privateers at Rhode Island that that goverment can not rule them, that sober men are in fear of their lives," was said in 1697. [b] The Bahamas were similarly involved in connivance at piracy; [c] nor were the Carolinas, Pennsylvania, and the Jerseys free from like suspicions. [d] Contumacy in regard to illegal trade, sheltering of pirates, and protection of deserters, as well as the reports of confusion and disorder in several of the colonies under proprietary charters brought the matter to a focus, and the sole question was in regard to the method by which the charters could best be vacated. The prosecution in the courts was a slow process, and the growth of belief

---

[a] B. of T. Papers, New England, Entry A, 134.

[b] B. of T. Papers, New England, Entry A, 156. Letter from Benjamin Davis, of Boston.

[c] The Dutch ambassador complained of these islands June 29, 1699. B. of T. Papers, Props., Entry A, 460.

[d] Ibid., Props., Entry B, 69, 33; Entry C, 29; Maryland B, 8; Pl. Genl., A, 11.

in Parliamentary omnipotence suggested that an act of that body would be the simplest and most efficacious mode of vacating these obnoxious instruments.[a]

BILL OF 1701.

The King's officers in the colonies, and the disaffected or discarded proprietary governors fostered the purpose of the board of trade by constant complaints.   Jeremiah Bass, a former governor of East Jersey, who was interestedly striving to destroy the proprietors' rights to government in that province in the hope of getting the King's commission for it, was a vigorous enemy of Penn and the Quaker proprieties.[b] Quary, who, as judge of the Pennsylvania Admiralty and the greatest merchant in the province, had his own profit to consider, desired to see Penn's charter confiscated.[c]   Dudley, who was scheming to be sent as governor to Massachusetts, and wished to include Rhode Island and Connecticut in his commission, was active against the charters.[d]   And, chief of all, Randolph, "prerogative's tool to Destroy the New England's charters,"[e] kept the matter before the board of trade.   From the time of Randolph's return to the colonies, after pushing through the navigation act of 1696, he continually made complaints of the proprietary governments, intimating that they were not only independent, but were talking of cutting loose and setting up for themselves;[f] that illegal trade could not be suppressed in the adjacent King's colonies as long as Connecticut, Rhode Island, the Jerseys, and Pennsylvania, "adjoining and intermixt" with these, enjoyed special privileges,[g] and that the King's revenue was thereby greatly diminished, which

---

a The board of trade represented to the House of Commons April 23, 1701: "Their independency making it absolutely necessary that some speedy and effectual care be taken to render them more subservient and useful to the Kingdom, which we conceive can not be otherwise well effected than by the legislative power of this Kingdom." B. of T. Papers, Pl. Genl., Entry B, 457. Penn wrote: "By nothing but downright Parliamentary omnipotency can my pretensions be overruled." Ibid., Props., G. 40.

b Pennsylvania Archives, I, 139.

c B. of T. Papers, Props., G, 40.

d Ashurst to Winthrop: "Dudley's going to New England, which hath been the bottom, of all." Mass. Hist. Colls., 6th series, III, 75.

e Letter of Penn. See Pennsylvania Archives, I, 139.

f Randolph to commissioners of customs, New Jersey Archives, 1st series, II, 116.

g B. of T. Papers, Pl. Genl., C. 18, August 25, 1698. Prince Society, Edward Randolph, V, 189-191.

mischief "will increase Till all the Proprieties are brought under his Maj[st] Imediate Governm[t]."[a]

When Randolph arrived in England late in 1700[b] he found already well under way the project of presenting to that session of Parliament a bill for "Re-uniting to the Crown the Governments of several Colonies and plantations in America."[c] He was at once employed in drawing up accusations, hunting up witnesses, and arranging for counsel.[d] On February 19, 1701, he presented a paper "setting forth the Misdemeanours and male Administration of Gov[rs] in y[e] Proprieties and Charter Govn[ts] of America,"[e] which, after citing the particular charges against the Bahama Islands, South Carolina, North Carolina, and Pennsylvania, Penn's lack of right to the three lower counties on the Delaware, the question as to the Jersey proprietorship, the faults of Connecticut, Rhode Island, and Massachusetts Bay, concludes: "These misdemeanors arise from proprietors not taking care to provide for the maintenance of their governors, so that honest men will not go out to live on the spoils and rapines of the proprieties;" that the proprietors have made no provision for defense, and that to suppress these growing evils the governments of all the proprieties should be vested in the Crown, saving all the rights of property in the land, as had already been done in the case of Maryland and New Hampshire.[f] March 5 Randolph presented another paper showing the bad conditions for defense, particularly in the proprietaries (the Quaker colonies of Pennsylvania and the Jerseys had no militia); and March 24 these two were combined into a paper marked "Articles of High Crimes: Misdemeanours Charged upon the Governours in the Severall Proprieties, on the Continent of America and

---

[a] B. of T. Papers, Pl. Genl., D, 48. Nov. 5, 1700. Prince Society, Edward Randolph, V, 239.

[b] Additional MSS. (British Museum) 9747, fo. 19. Letter to Blathwait. Penn indicated that Randolph's influence was on the wane about this time. See Pennsylvania Archives, I, 139.

[c] B. of T. Papers, Props., I, 16, gives text of the bill.

[d] Ashurst shows that the matter was a surprise. July 10, 1701, he wrote: "After I had pressed to be heard about y[r] boundaries and also about y[r] appeales, and that I might have Councill * * * I was told they were busy & could not attend to it. I thought then there was something a brewing by y[r] old friends M[r] D. & M[r] Rand: and one Bass came in that was to doe all y[r] businies at once, by continuing this Act of Parl., a copie whereof is here enclosed." Mass. Hist. Colls., 6th series, iii, 75.

[e] B. of T. Papers, Props., F, 69.

[f] Ibid. A portion printed in N. C. Col. Recs., I, 545.

Islands adjacent."[a]   Two days later the board of trade made
a representation to the King in council to the following effect:[b]

Having formerly on severall occasions humbly represented to your Majesty
the state of the Government under Proprietors and Charters in America;
and perceiving the irregularities of these Governments dayly to increase,
to the prejudice of Trade, and of your Majesties other Plantations in
America, as well as of your Majesties revenue arising from the Customes
here, we find ourselves obliged at present humbly to represent to your
Majesty;

That those Colonies in general have no ways answered the chief design
for which such large Tracts of Land and such Priviledges and Immunities
were granted by the Crown.

That they have not conformed themselves to the severall acts of Parliament for regulating Trade and Navigation, to which they ought to pay the
same obedience, and submit to the same Restrictions as the other Plantations, which are subject to your Majesties immediate Government, on the
contrary in most of these Proprieties and Charter Governments, the Governours have not applyed themselves to your Majesty for your approbation, nor have taken the Oaths required by the acts of Trade, both which
Qualifications are made necessary by the late Act for preventing frauds
and regulating abuses in the Plantation Trade.

That they have assumed to themselves a power to make Laws contrary
and repugnant to the Laws of England, and directly prejudicial to Trade,
some of them having refused to send hither such Laws as they had
enacted, and others having sent them but very imperfectly.

That diverse of them have denyed appeals to your Majesty in Councill,
oy which not only the Inhabitants of those Colonies but others your
Majesties subjects are deprived of that benefit, enjoyed in the Plantations,
under your Majesties immediate Government, and the parties agrieved
are left without remedy from the arbitrary and Illegal proceedings of
their Courts.

That these Colonies continue to be the refuge and retreat of Pirates &
Illegal Traders, and the receptacle of Goods imported thither from for-
reign parts contrary to Law: In return of which Commodities those of the
growth of these Colonies are likewise contrary to Law exported to For-
reign parts; All which is likewise much incouraged by their not admitting
appeals as aforesaide.

That by raising and lowering their coin from time to time, to their particular advantage, and to the prejudice of other Colonies, By exempting
their Inhabitants from Duties and Customes to which the other Colonies
are subject, and by Harbouring of Servants and fugitives, these Governments tend greatly to the undermining the Trade and Welfare of the other
Plantations, and seduce and draw away the People thereof; By which
Diminution of Hands the rest of the Colonies more beneficial to England
do very much suff[r]

---

[a] B. of T. Papers, Props., G, 3.   Printed in New Jersey Archives, first series, II, 358; also
Prince Society, Edward Randolph, v, 263–268.

[b] B. of T. Papers, Props., Entry C, 12.   Printed in N. C. Col. Recs., I, 535.

That these Independent Colonies do turn the Course of Trade to the Promoting and proprogating woolen and other Manufactures proper to England, instead of applying their thoughts and Endeavours to the production of such commodities as are fit to be encouraged in these parts according to the true design and intention of such settlements.[a]

That they do not in general take any due care for their own defence and security against an Enemy, either in Building Forts or providing their Inhabitants with sufficient Armes and Amunition, in case they should be attacked, which is every day more and more to be apprehended, considering how the French pow^r encreases in those parts.

That this cheifly arises from the ill use they make of the powers entrusted to them by their Charters, and the Independency which they pretend to, and that each Government is obliged only to defend its self without any consideration had of their Neighbours, or of the general preservation of the whole.

That many of them have not a regular militia and some (particularly the Colonies of East and West New Jersey) are no otherwise at present than in a state of Anarchy and confusion.

And because the care of these and other great mischiefs in your Majesties Plantations and Colonies aforesaid, and the introducing such an administration of Government and fit regulation of Trade as may put them into a better State of Security and make them duly subservient and usefull to England, does every day become more and more necessary, and that your Majesties frequent Commands to them have not met with due complyance: We humbly conceive it may be expedient that the Charters of the severall Proprietors and others intitling them to absolute Government be reassumed to the Crown and these Colonies put into the same State and dependency as those of your Majesties other Plantations, without prejudice to any man's particular property and freehold. Which being no otherwise so well to be effected as by the Legislative power of this Kingdome.

Wee humbly submit the same to your Majesties Royal consideration.

The King, in council, having determined to accept the advice of the board of trade, the bill was introduced into the House of Lords, April 24, 1701, and ordered to its second reading the next week.[b] This bill provided for declaring void all clauses of the charters of Massachusetts Bay, New Hampshire, Rhode Island, and Providence Plantations, Connecticut in New England, East and West New Jersey, Pennsylvania and the adjacent Territories (Delaware), Maryland, Carolina, and the Bahama or Luca Islands in America, relating to the government, whereby any power or authority is granted to any person or persons from the Crown.

---

[a] Larkin wrote: "I have seen as good Druggits of that countries make [Connecticut and Rhode Island] sold at 4 sh. and 4 sh. 6d. per yard as ever I saw in England in my life." B. of T. Papers, Maryland, Entry, B, 115."

[b] Journals of the House of Lords, XVII, 659b.

On the same day the board of trade presented to the House
of Commons a full list of the irregularities and misdemeanors
of the various charter and proprietary governments.   Each
one in turn was complained of—Rhode Island, for her recep-
tion of Lord Bellamont's inquiry into her irregularities and
for "pretending by their charter to be independent of the
Government of England;" Connecticut, for refusing the Hallam
appeal and for the public declaration of her governor that
no appeals should be allowed from thence; the Jerseys, for
their utter confusion and unlawful trade; Pennsylvania, for
opposition to the courts of Admiralty and for illegal trade, as
represented by Colonel Quary;[a] the Carolinas and Bahamas
for the misbehavior of their governors and harboring pirates.
As to the proprietary and charter governments in general,
"their independency making it absolutely necessary that
some speedy and effectual Care be taken to render them more
subservient and useful to this Kingdom," they propose the
aforementioned bill.

This bill took the proprietors unawares.   The board of trade
employed Randolph to lobby for the Government,[b] and he was
prepared with numerous witnesses and documents to push the
bill forward.   The first protest came from William Penn, jr.,
whose father, absent in Pennsylvania, was unable to use his
influence, and who had no idea that the covert attacks upon
his charter would take this form.[c] His son petitioned that
"the Act seems to take away the estate of the Petitioner's
father purchased from the Crown for a valuable consideration."[d] An order was given that he should be heard.   Sir
Henry Ashurst, the agent whom the Connecticut colony had
been fortunate enough to appoint in February of this same
year, for the matter of the Hallam appeal and the boundary
dispute, used his utmost endeavors and his large influence

---

[a] He complained that "iron, linnen, wine, and other European commodities are sold
there as cheap as in England."

[b] B. of T. Papers, Pl. Genl., entry C, 47.   Prince Society, Edward Randolph, V, 273, 274.
Letter to Lords of the Treasury to furnish Randolph with money, as the board of trade had
given him orders to follow the matter for the Crown.   His bill is a curious document,
including amounts spent on the witnesses, "keeping them together in the old palace
yard, 5sh., 8d.; dining them the same dayse, £2, 8sh., 12d.; keeping witnesses together,
8sh., 6d.," etc.   Sum total, £96, 11s. 6d.   P. R. O.   Treasury Papers, LXXV, 8.

[c] Penn wrote, in 1700, "At what a pass, then, are proprietary Gov[mts], who unless they
will run their heads ag[st] the wall are in danger of being quo warranto'd by the late Act
ag[st] Piracy."

[d] Journal of House of Lords, XVI, 660b.

to defeat the passage of the bill.   May 5 he wrote: "I am soliciting the Lords day and night that if the bill must pass, to leave out yor Colony; you have this reputation none of the Coloneys hath, a person of my quality to appear for them."^a Persons of still higher quality were concerned in opposition— the proprietors of the Carolinas and Bahamas—but they made a rather languid defense, being present by counsel and in the person of their secretary but once.   Possibly they were not averse to being relieved of the government of these tumul- tuous and unprofitable possessions.   Lord Baltimore, although not exercising his proprietary right in Maryland, was repre- sented by counsel; but the brunt of the defense fell upon the Penns and Sir Henry Ashurst.

The second reading was set for April 29, but postponed until May 8.   Meanwhile Randolph poured in papers from the Admiralty, the commissioners of customs, and the board of trade,^b summoned witnesses, and tried every possible influ- ence to promote the speedy passage of the bill.   Its second reading was passed May 23.   During the course of the cam- paign, Randolph intimated that his enemies were threatening him with arrest, and requested the protection of the House, which was granted.^c   But the pressure of the near proroguing of Parliament was too much even for the persistency and zeal of Randolph.   June 11, after the third reading had been post- poned four times, he reported to the board that there was no probability of the passage of the bill at this session, and requested permission to take the affidavits of several witnesses for future use.^d   Ashurst intimated in a letter to the Connec- ticut governor that he used a certain interest he possessed in the House of Lords to have the bill delayed,^e but declares that they must send over some one to defend it in the next session.

The early dissolution of Parliament, on the departure of the King for Ireland, checked but in no wise disconcerted the board and the promoters of the bill.   It only served as a pre-

^a Mass. Hist. Colls., 6th series, III, 62. Sir Henry enlarged upon the value of his serv- ices, but there was much danger that the bill would pass the House of Lords, at least.
^b Secretary Popple drew up a list of complaints of each colony stretching back for some years. B. of T Papers, Props., entry C, 67.
^c Journal of House of Lords, XVI, 686b.
^d B. of T. Papers, Journal F, 85.
^e Mass. Hist. Colls., 6th series, III, 75. Saltonstall thinks Ashurst's methods would bet- ter be kept quiet or they might prove disadvantageous to the colony.

lude to further efforts. July 16, 1701, Bass presented a memorial suggesting a commission of investigation into the state of proprietary and charter governments.[a] Thereupon the board ordered letters to be sent to Governor Blakiston in Maryland and Governor Nicholson in Virginia to get proofs of the charges, and the same instructions to be given to Dudley, Cornbury, and Randolph, who were preparing to go to America.[b] In the letter to Blakiston they said: "The bill, by reason of shortness of time and the multiplicity of other business, not having passed into an act, and it being very probable that the same matter may again come under consideration the next session, you are instructed,"[c] etc. Ashurst wrote, November 1, 1701, to his Connecticut clients: "You must be prepared against another attempt upon yor charter by Act of Parl. Insolvent Randall (Randolph) & D. & another nameless friend[d] was and are very active gentlemen against all proprietary governments."[e] Penn wrote: "Those who seek to ruin the proprietaries, they say, will renew their bill, but try the Commons first."[f] Penn himself made vigorous efforts to defeat the bill, raising a subscription among the Quakers in Pennsylvania to be used against it.[g] In 1702 he wrote: "The Jersey's surrender is an ugly preface, however there is a higher hand to which I look.[h] The Lords of Trade have promised me to receive no complaints without the party sending them give them to the party they are sent against upon the spot * * * that no body may be murdered in the dark. A great reformative relief and for which American governments owe me their good will."[i]

Even the good offices of Ashurst and Penn proved unavailing; the charters were to be placed in jeopardy once more. The board continued to represent the defenseless state of these colonies, which, in view of imminent war, was a serious charge, and in February, 1702, one of the secretaries of state sent the

a B. of T. Papers, Props., G, 22.

b Ibid., Journal F, 107.

c B. of T. Papers, Maryland, Entry B, 86.

d Lord Cornbury, without doubt.

e Mass. Hist. Colls., 6th series, III, 85.

f Penn to Logan, January 4, 1702.

g B. of T. Papers, Pl. Gen'l, E, 31.

h Quary claimed that Penn trusted his influence at court to carry through all his measures.

i Janney, Life of Penn (Philadelphia, 1883), p. 458.

board the heads of a new bill.[a]   It proposed that the military government by sea and land should be reunited to the Crown, that the person deputed by the King as commander in chief should superintend the customs and admiralty officers, that the civil authority and administration should rest where they were (as they did in corporations in England where the King had his governors); but that justice should run in the King's name, appeals above £300 value lie to him, and he should have a negative on all laws.   Had the board of trade been content with these reasonable and moderate proposals, which a few years before they would have considered as embodying their policy, it is quite probable that such a bill could have been carried.   But the board replied that they were not "adapted to Proprieties in Generall nor are they proper for Pennsylvania in particular," that the chief ends proposed were to render the colonies mutually defensive, to suppress illegal trade and piracy, and prevent the escape of fugitives, "and that the Produce of the whole should be turned to the Benefit of England."   This they thought could not be accomplished by these propositions, and they preferred the bill of the last session.[b] They were considering this matter for several days, and February 23 a counselor of the treasury informed the board that he had been directed to solicit the bill.[c]   But on March 3 the King unexpectedly died and Parliament was dissolved.   This sudden turn of affairs and the downfall of the Tory ministry put an end to the first attempt at a wholesale confiscation of the charters by Parliamentary action.

THE INFLUENCE OF THE ENGLISH CHURCH.

The bill of 1701 was but a prelude to a second and more persistent attack upon the corporation and proprietary governments.   It had formed an excellent precedent, had called attention to the misdemeanors of these governments, and had raised up a large crop of avaricious enemies, who hoped to exploit these colonies to their own advantage.   After his failure to lobby through the bill of 1701,[d] Edward Randolph seems

---

[a] B. of T. Papers, Props., H, 13.

[b] B. of T. Papers, Props., Entry C, 383.

[c] Ibid., Journal F, 336, 338.

[d] B. of T. Papers, Journals, show that after his final return to America his reports were shelved. He died in 1703, and was buried on the eastern shore of Virginia.

to have fallen into disrepute with the board. But his place both as surveyor-general of customs in America and as opponent in chief of the corporation and proprietary governments was actively filled by Robert Quary, formerly governor for a brief time of South Carolina, later judge of the Admiralty in Pennsylvania.[a]

Lord Cornbury, the dissolute heir of the Earl of Clarendon and cousin of the queen, had been appointed the new governor of New York, and Joseph Dudley,[b] the renegade Puritan, had been placed in charge of Massachusetts. Both looked with envious eyes on the two small but thriving colonies east and south of their respective governments, and set systematically to work to abolish the charters of these colonies and annex their territories to their commands.[c] Cornbury had already been gratified by an additional commission for the government of the two Jerseys, whose proprietors had made a forced surrender of their governmental rights to the Crown.[d] "We hear that the latter (the Jerseys) have surrendered their government to the King, which will be a leading case to the rest," wrote an inhabitant of Pennsylvania to the governor of Maryland at this time.[e] In a word, all those who were "gaping for preferment under the specious pretense of serving the King's interest"[f] were looking to the downfall of the corporation and proprietary colonies as their best chance and inciting the enmity of the board of trade by continued accusations.

A plan seems to have been on foot to introduce a bill for the overthrow of the charters in Queen Anne's first Parliament, of December, 1702; but the board wrote to Dudley January 26, 1703, that "the time is too far spent to expect it

---

[a] In South Carolina Quary was accused of complicity with pirates and deposed from his governorship (Historical Collections of South Carolina, I, 86). Possibly this accounts for his opposition to proprietaries. McCrady tries to clear him of the charge; but his record in Pennsylvania was not flawless.

[b] Ashurst claimed he might have prevented Dudley's appointment had he been commissioned to do so. Mass. Hist. Colls., 6th series, III, 39.

[c] Dudley's "son declared to a gentleman in his company at Stoningtown that within a year my Ld Cornbury would make 2 of his Commission^rs (both of this province [Connecticut] & who had shown themselves with the greatest heat ag^t. the interests of this Government) magistrates of this government, but we hope he will prove as false a prophet as accuser." Governor and council of Connecticut to Sir Henry Ashurst, August 29, 1705. Mass. Hist. Colls., 6th series, III, 304.

[d] See Chapter II, ante.

[e] B. of T. Papers, Props., K, 44.

[f] Ibid., Props., G., 40, letter of William Penn,

from this present session."[a] In order, however, that the matter should be kept prominent, every possible opportunity was seized for presenting the project to the notice of the Queen in council. For example, in a representation on the subject of governors' salaries, April 2, 1703, the board concludes:

As to Proprietary and Charter Colonies, viz. Rhode Island, Connecticut, Pennsylvania, Carolina, and the Bahama Islands we cannot propose anything upon this occasion. The governours of those colonies not being appointed by your Maj'ty, and depending upon the proprietors or People from whom they have mean uncertain salaries, which encourages them to connive at unlawful trade and other irregularities which mischief can only be remedied as we humbly conceive by reducing these colonies to an immediate dependence on the Crown. [b]

Thus the people of the corporation colonies as well as the proprietors were kept in anxiety concerning their charter rights and privileges. William Penn, after a hard fight with Quary before the board concerning the admiralty powers in his government, realized the temper of that body as adverse to all proprietary governments, and decided to follow the example of his New Jersey friends, and by making his own terms of surrender to get out of the difficulty before his charter was annulled in Parliament. May 11, 1703, he wrote to the board:

"Hon[able] Friends Since I observe your bent is extreamly strong to bring all proprietary Governments more immediately under the disposition of the Crown and the disadvantage they are and must be under on that account, I thought fit to lett you know that upon a just regard for the security of me and the people in our Civil rights * * * I shall upon satisfaction resigne to the Crown the Government thereof." [c]

With Penn, therefore, showing signs of yielding, with the pressure for union caused by the new French war, and the complete loss of the proprietary colony of the Bahamas, captured and sacked by the French and Spaniards in June and again in September, 1703,[d] and with the return to power in England of the Tory party,

---

[a] B. of T. Papers, New England, Entry D, 374.

[b] Privy Council Register, 1701-4, p. 356.

[c] B. of T. Papers, Props., L, 28. See ante, ch. 2.

[d] Ibid., Props., M. 2. A letter describing the capture of the Bahamas says: "These islands were out of the Queen's protection and independent of the Crown (one of the ill effects of Charters) * * * I hope this will induce the Queen to take that Government (and all the rest for they lye alike exposed) into her immediate protection. The naked and defenseless posture of the Proprieties in gen'll are unanswerable motives were there no others."

which believed in prerogative and supported the projects of the governors of New York and Massachusetts,[a] there seemed few chances for the continuation of governments under charters.

In addition to all these forces set in motion against the charter colonies, another agency was acting powerfully in opposition to them, because they were the homes and refuges of dissenters from the Church of England. Queen Anne was a devout and rigid supporter of the Establishment, and the English Dissenters, who had been tolerated and protected under William III, were being hard pressed by the test act and the occasional conformity bill. Meanwhile their colonial brethren, so long the dominant class in New England, New York, Pennsylvania, the Jerseys, and the Carolinas, found the powerful engine of the church establishment in use against their privileges and liberties.[b]

Up to this time but few congregations of the Church of England had been organized in the Independent and Quaker colonies. King's Chapel, Boston, was a relic of the era of Andros. Christ Church, Philadelphia, founded in 1695, was an active center of the opposition to the Quaker ascendency and the proprietors' government.[c] About the beginning of the reign of Queen Anne a new impetus was given to the Church of England party in the colonies by the organization for work therein of a missionary society known as the "Society for the Propagation of the Gospel." Its charter, granted in 1701, recites that, being informed that the provision for ministers in many of the plantations beyond the seas is very mean, and that many English subjects lack the administration of the sacrament, this organization has been incorporated to remedy such condition of affairs.[d] The first meeting was held at Lambeth June 27, and August 15 the society entered upon an inquiry into the religious state of the colonies, seeking information from colonial governors, from merchants,

---

[a] Cornbury's uncle, Lord Rochester, was a member of the Tory cabinet of 1702. Blathwait was Dudley's patron.

[b] Penn wrote, August 26, 1901. "Nor is it the powers of Govm't alone that is here contended for. Liberties and the first inducem[ts] to undertake so hazardous and difficult an Enterprise are struck at by that Bill, and must inevitably fall if carried on upon the bottom it now stands." B. of T. Papers, Props., G., 40.

[c] B. of T. Papers, Props., G., 13. Petitions from the vestry of Christ Church complaining of the unjust discrimination against the Church of England on the part of Penn and the Assembly.

[d] Abstract of Charter (1702), British Museum pamphlet.

and from the board of trade. Dudley furnished the information for New England, and Col. Lewis Morris for the Jerseys and Pennsylvania.[a] The report of 1702 says that "first
having got the best information they could of the present
state of the Christian religion in our American Plantations
they find that in some places it is so sad and deplorable that
there are scarce any footsteps of Religion to be seen among
them."[b] In consequence the Rev. George Keith, with the
Rev. Patrick Gordon, were sent out as itinerant missionaries,
on the same ship with Dudley and Morris.[c] Morris wrote
about this time, "If the Church can be settled in New
England it pulls up schisme in America by the roots, that
being the fountain that supplies with infectious streame all
the rest of America."[d]

In Boston, Dudley[e] seems to have played a double part,
often attending King's Chapel and taking pains to let the
authorities in England know of his zeal for the Established
Church, while on the other hand he curried favor with the
Congregational party by assuring them that at heart he was
still an Independent, and by continuing his membership in
the church of his fathers.[f] In New York, Lord Cornbury
attempted to prove his zeal for the Queen's service by
supporting the Establishment, and forcing laws upon the
assembly for the payment of Church of England clergymen,
combined with a petty persecution of the dissenting sects,
especially the Puritans upon Long Island.[g] In Pennsylvania,
Quary was the leader of the Church party, and was using its
influence to overthrow the proprietary government.[h] It was
at this time, also, that the High Church party in South Caro-

---

a Digest of the Society (3d edition, 1892).

b Account of the Society (1706), British Museum pamphlet.

c S. P. G.—A. MSS., I, 9. Keith, Travels (London, 1706).

d S. P. G.—A. MSS., I, 45.

e Ibid., I, 9. Keith wrote, June 12, 1702: "Our worthy friend Governour Dudley is well
* * * his Conversation [on the voyage] was both pleasant and instructive insomuch
that the great Cabin of the ship was like a Colledge for good Discourse in matters Theo-
logical and Philosophical, and very cordially he joined with us in divine worship, and I
well understand he purposeth to give All possible encouragement to the Congregation of
the Church of England in this place [Boston]."

f Palfrey, History of New England, IV, 297.

g S. P. G.—A. MSS. I, 50, 54, 105.

h In 1704 the vestry of Christ Church, Philadelphia, petitioned Cornbury to persuade
the Queen to take over the government of Pennsylvania, and appoint him governor.
Penn charged that this was done by a packed vestry. (B. of T. Papers, Props., M, 22.)
Keith was also making complaints and charges against the "great deficiency of Quaker
Government." (S. P. G.—A. MSS., I, 89, 103, 119, 121; II, 23.)

lina, relying upon the support of the palatine, endeavored to drive the Dissenters from the assembly. The inhabitants of this colony were vigorously protesting against this policy, and the Society for the Propagation of the Gospel appointed a committee to act with the Archbishop of Canterbury and the Bishop of London in the House of Lords. Not until afterwards did the members learn that they had thus unwittingly played into the hands of the Dissenting party.[a] All this indicates that the new society was mixing in politics, and that its influence would be exerted in favor of the revocation of charter rights and the appointment of royal governors who would be zealous for the Church Establishment.

Events in Connecticut were typical. In 1703 the society reported that "In all the Provinces east of New York there are no Church of England congregations, neither in Connecticut, Narragansett, Plimouth, New Hampshire or Mayne, except at Boston." In 1704 Colonel Heathcote, of New York, who had a manor house on the borders of Connecticut, was elected a member of the Society for the Propagation of the Gospel, and, being a zealous churchman, looked about to see what could be done to further its interests in his neighborhood. November 9, 1705, he wrote a long letter to the society describing the colony of Connecticut and the opportunity it afforded for missionary labors.

There is no place on the Continent from whence ye church can have so fair an Opportunity to make Impressions upon ye Dissenters as in that Government. * * * It contains in length about 140 miles and has in it about 40 towns in each of which there is a Presbyterian or Independent Minister settled by their Law. * * * They have an abundance of odd kind of Laws to prevent any Disenting from their Church and they look upon the Church as their most dangerous enemy. More than half the people think our Church to be little better than the Papist.

He admits that the work will be difficult and will meet with bitter opposition, but thinks the people should be undeceived in regard to the church and have an opportunity to have their children baptized.[b] In accordance with his suggestion, he and a Mr. Muirson, a missionary of the society settled at Rye, N. Y., went on an itinerary into Connecticut, both of them

<hr>

[a] S. P. G.—A. MSS., II, 68, 149; III, 152. See Chap. II, ante, the Carolinas.
[b] S. P. G., A. MSS., II, 117.

being fully armed. Colonel Heathcote wrote to the society
that "their ministers were very uneasy at our coming and
abundance of pains were taken to persuade & terrify the
people from hearing Mr. Muirson but it availed nothing." [a]
It is probable that but for the support and presence of so
considerable a gentleman as Colonel Heathcote the Church
of England missionary might have been imprisoned. [b] On his
second coming into the colony there was a still greater com-
motion. "One of the Magistrates with some other Officers
came to my Lodgings on Saturday and in the hearing of
Colonel Heathcote and a great many people read a long
paper. The meaning of it was to let me know that theirs
was a Charter Government that I had done an *illegal* thing
in coming among them to establish new ways of worship,"
wrote Mr. Muirson to the secretary, [c] complaining in detail
of these laws, "which being repugnant to the Laws of England is contrary to the grant of their Charter. And which I
humbly presume if our Gracious Queen was acquainted with
Her Maj'ty wou'd be pleased to disannull the same, or at least
make it ineffectual against the settling the Nationall Church."
The society took immediate steps to secure the repeal of this
law, [d] entitled "Ecclesiastical," but recommended gentle
means to their missionary. [e] Thereupon Colonel Heathcote
replied:

> It would be a great breach of prudence and discretion to act otherwise
> for we are here in an enemies country and by the Laws they pretend to
> govern themselves: Independency & Presbytery are the established
> Churches and the Church of England the only Dissenters and indeed the
> only people they unwillingliest wou'd admit to have Liberty of Conscience
> amongst them. [f] I am sorry any body shou'd be so unjust in giving the
> Society an Acct of ye people of this Colony as that they are a well mean-
> ing & not a heady people, nothing being more true than the contrary.

That the opposition of the Connecticut people to the Church
of England missionary was due in part to their fear that it
would militate against the continuance of their charter seems

---

[a] S. P. G., A. MSS., II, 165.

[b] Ibid., III, 156, 173. Colonel Heathcote was being urged for governor of New York,
and the Society for the Propagation of the Gospel was supporting him.

[c] S. P. G., A. MSS., III, 76; April 14, 1707.

[d] S. P. G., Journal, I, 127.

[e] Ibid., A. MSS., III, 168.

[f] Ibid., A. MSS., III, 187.

evident from a letter to the secretary of the society, somewhat
later (July 25, 1710):

> By this conveyance come some papers from Connecticut * * * there
> want not those who say there are some entertain hopes of overturning the
> Government, and *wou'd use the Church as an engine to do it*, how true that
> is I dare not say. [a]

BILL OF 1706.

The active opposition of the ecclesiastical authorities, added
to the private schemes of the governors of Massachusetts and
New York, the public accusations of the customs officials,[b]
and the strong desire of the board of trade to produce uniformity in colonial administration, led to new attempts to
introduce into Parliament a bill to destroy all colonial
charters.

Dudley had brought over with him a commission similar to
Lord Bellomont's to command the Connecticut militia[c] and
also that of Rhode Island. As soon as he had arranged affairs
in Boston he went on to Rhode Island to publish this commission.[d] Thereupon "the Quakers raged indecently, saying
they were ensnared and injured," and refused his right to review the militia, signifying "they would rather lose all at
once than by pieces," and insisting that, by their charter,
power of the militia was granted them. Dudley intimated
that the majority of the people would pray to be taken under
the Queen's government, but dared not. The board in consequence helped on his scheme by representing that, this being
an "extraordinary exigency," Dudley should be appointed
governor.[e] The petition of the colony in justification of their
action was presented by William Penn, who served them as
agent in this emergency, and by whose influence the danger
of a royal governor was averted.

Dudley then accused Rhode Island of opposition to the
Admiralty court, and secured the repeal of an act of the Rhode
Island assembly, whereby they claimed Admiralty jurisdic-

---

[a] S. P. G., A. MSS., v. 143. A church was founded at Stratford, with Muirson as pastor,
but after his death, in 1709, no missionary was appointed for Connecticut until 1722.

[b] Representation of a custom-house official in New York, June 26, 1703: "All the labor
and industry in the proprietary governments is of no advantage to the Crown." Harleian
MSS. (British Museum), 6273, No. 1.

[c] Ashurst secured a restriction in that of Connecticut, that the militia was only to be
called out for Connecticut's defense. Mass. Hist. Colls., 6th series, III, 119.

[d] B. of T. Papers, New England, Entry D, 285.

[e] Ibid., Props., Entry D, 244.

tion. [a] His claim that they had refused to allow the condemnation of a valuable prize ship that had been captured by a
privateer[b] and brought into Newport awoke a chorus of indig-
nation against Dudley, who had declined to condemn the prize
without a bribe of £50 from the owners of the privateer.[c]
The testimony of the Admiralty officers in favor of the colony
made him drop this charge in regard to the Admiralty for
others that could be better substantiated. The irregularity
most likely to be condemnatory was that concerning war and
defense. Dudley complained that seamen and impressed
soldiers escaped by scores to the charter governments, which
refused all assistance in times of extreme danger. [d] Cornbury
put in the same charges against Connecticut, "who will not
raise a Quota until they have applied to the Queen & received
her answer."[e] He urged the confiscation of their charter on
this ground, and because they filled Long Island with contra-
band goods, and the people of the east end of that island chafed
at belonging to New York and were " full of New England
principles." He wrote, September, 1703, that Rhode Island
and Connecticut would not furnish their quota until compelled
to, either by some act of Parliament or such other method as
the Queen shall use. "They hate anybody that owns subjection to the Queen. That our people find every day; for if
any of our merchants of this place goes to sue for a just debt
in the court of Connecticut, to be sure he shall have no right
if his suite is against one of that colony."[f] Dudley represented
that, taxes being much lower in these colonies, many inhabitants of Massachusetts were enticed away and the prosecution
of the war suffered.[g] All these charges were successively
represented to the Queen by the board[h] and led to the attempt
to appoint royal governors for these colonies in 1704.[i] Sir
Henry Ashurst wrote concerning these charges: " I am sence-

---

a B. of T. Papers, Props., M 3. The Board of Trade suggested that the passage of such
an act was sufficient to justify forfeiture of their charter, but the attorney-general decided
otherwise.
b Ibid., New England, M, 37; Entry E, 92.
c B. of T. Papers, New England, P. 36, 37.
d Ibid., New England, N, 22, 38; Entry E, 346.
e Ibid., New York, W, 27, 28, 30.
f Ibid., New York, W, 30, Printed N. Y. Col. Docs., IV,. 1070.
g Ibid., New England, N, 38.
h Representations of Board of Trade, July 16, 1703, B. of T. Papers, New England, Entry
E, 92; Jan. 13, 1704, B. of T. Papers, Props., Entry D, 403; Feb. 16, 1704, B. of T. Papers,
New England, Entry E, 206; July 10, 1704, Ibid., New England, Entry E, 358.
i See ante, ch. 3.

able Dud: & Co. doe complain of yor not sending yor quota that they may put the money in their pocketts.^{a} * * * There is nothing of his complaints but strickes at the Gouverment, and therefore the Generall Assembly ought so to take it; and if once you are hectored or worried out of yor gouvernment, then fairwel to yor libertyes."^{b}

Failing in the attempt to secure the governorship of these colonies by executive action, the board revived the old project of a bill against all the charters, and sent to the governors of New York and Massachusetts to serve notice on the governors of Rhode Island and Connecticut and to produce evidence and depositions of witnesses to prove their charges.^{c} The charges were a repetition of the previous ones, that these colonies broke the acts of trade, harbored pirates, concealed deserters, refused quotas for the war, protected debtors, forbade the laws of England to be pleaded in their courts, denied appeals, rejected the vice-admiralty commissions and commissions to command their militia.^{d} In addition, Rhode Island was charged with disrespect and contumely toward Governor Dudley, and Connecticut with having an ecclesiastical law "which extends even to the Church of England."^{e} The charges against the two small corporation colonies were received by Dudley and Cornbury in July, 1705, and they at once took every means at hand to procure proof of all past misdemeanors of Rhode Island and Connecticut. Both complain of the difficulty of procuring evidence, "lesser persons being afraid to be known to attend me, alledging they cannot live in their province in peace, if it once be known they have given evidence against."^{f} After three months' persistency Dudley sent over his affidavits in proof of his charges, saying that he hopes they are very plain, that he has taken all manner of pains with them.^{g} An examination of the proofs shows the slight foundation on

^{a} The charges against Dudley for taking bribes were not confined to this occasion. See Mass Hist. Colls., 6th series, III, 384.

^{b} Mass. Hist. Colls., 6th series, III, 298.

^{c} B. of T. Papers, Props., N, 42, April 18, 1705; Journal, I, 361

^{d} B. of T. Papers, Props., Entry D, 134; Entry E, 140. Printed in R. I. Col. Recs., IV, 14.

^{e} This was part of the Society for the Propagation of the Gospel's activity.

^{f} B. of T. Papers, New England, P, 68; Dudley to the Board, November 1, 1705. Cornbury wrote that the magistrates frightened the people from coming to him. Ibid., New York, V, 22.

^{g} Ibid., New England, P, 68, 77.

which such a superstructure of charges was built. In reply
to the thirteen specific charges, Dudley secured the testimony
of but two men, James Menzies, "a practioner in the Rhode
Island" courts, evidently one of his tools, and Nathaniel Coddington, who had a personal grievance against the Rhode
Island government. [a] In rebuttal of the serious charges
made against them, the Rhode Island government took immediate steps for their own defense. They appointed an English
Quaker, Wharton, as their agent, and sent him an answer in
detail, which was duly presented to the board. [b] Most of the
charges they stoutly denied. In regard to the quota, they
had been informed by counsel learned in law that they were not
obliged to furnish a quota to other provinces; nevertheless
they have done so and their militia did good service in
defending the frontier. They were also a "frontier by sea,"
and had raised large taxes for fortifications.

Cornbury and Dudley furnished the Connecticut government, at its request, with a list of the charges against them.
Winthrop courteously replied to Dudley that "it happens
well they are fallen in your hands, who as I know you can, soe
I hope you will certify to their Lordships they are wholly
groundless." [c] But Dudley sent over a list of proofs, [d] including Hallam and Palmes's appeal case, and charges that Connecticut had refused a quota for the war. Cornbury's affidavits
in regard to Connecticut are interesting. He inclosed a book
of their laws, marking several as being repugnant to the laws
of England, and saying that the first law abrogates all the laws
of England at once. [e] He inclosed a long list of depositions [f]
proving the ecclesiastical arrangements for town rates for the
minister's salary, and that no other service except that authorized was permitted. For the breach of this rule two men
were then in gaol. He inclosed many papers that had been
used in the Hallam appeal case, and even brought up the harboring of the regicides, Whalley and Goffe, after the Restora-
ation of 1660. A certain Sackett testified that he was talking
with the high sheriff of New London, who said "that they
had nothing to doe with the Queen nor ye Queen hath nothing

a Dudley's affidavits are in B. of T. Papers, Props., O, 12, 13, 14.
b Ibid., Props., O, 27.
c Ibid., 19.
d Ibid., 20.
e B. of T. Papers, New York, V, 22.
f B. of T. Papers, Props., O, 39–47.

to doe with them for they would Loose their Lives before
they would loose their privileges except the Queen herselfe
came to Demand it."[a]   And at New Haven he had heard one
say that "they would never loose their Charter and their priviledges, they would first Loose their Lives or words to that
effect."[b]   The captain of the fort at Saybrook said that "if
ye Queen sent any of her officers to take away any of their
privileges that they had Good arms and men to Defend themselves and would doe it, and would serve them worse than ever
S[r] Edmund Andros ye late Gov[r] of New York was served."[b]

Meanwhile the difficulty with the Mohegan Indians arose,
which was to drag on so many weary years, and this increased
the colony's jeopardy.[c]   It was a land-grabbing scheme con-
cocted by Dudley and his associates, and entered into by the
disappointed Palmes and Hallam, of the appeal case.   The
Indian sachem, Owaneco, son and heir of Unca, who stood by
the colony in the Pequot war, was prevailed upon to consider
himself and his tribe as wronged by the appropriation of their
lands by the Connecticut government and to deed his title in
these lands to the aforementioned gentlemen.   They thereupon conveyed Owaneco to London, where he posed as an
Indian prince, and his wrongs were commented upon and
enlarged.   Blathwayt, one of the board of trade, became
Owaneco's patron,[d] and succeeded in getting a commission
appointed to investigate the Indians' claims on the ground.
It was to be composed of the chief enemies of the colony and
presided over by Dudley.[e]   In August, 1705, he came down to
Stonington in great state, and, arrogantly refusing to notify
the colonial government, held the court of commission against
the protest of the Connecticut authorities.[f]   After a pretended
inquiry, which examined the evidence for one side only (the
Connecticut authorities forbade the recognition of the jurisdiction of the commission), a verdict was given in the
Indians' favor, and judgment was pronounced that the colony
should immediately vacate their lands and pay the costs of the

---

a B. of T. Papers, Props., O. 47.
b Ibid.
c See "Mohegan Land Controversy," New Haven Historical Society Papers, III, 205;
also "Talcott Papers," Connecticut Historical Society Collections, IV.   The case was not
settled until 1771.
d Mass. Hist. Colls., 6th series, III, 378.
e Commission empowered March 3, 1704.
f B. of T. Papers, Props., O, 8; S., 67, give a full rehearsal of the case.

investigation. These were placed at the enormous sum of £573 12s. 8d.[a] Dudley also complained of insolent treatment by the colonial authorities, and his letters, reaching England at this same time, insinuated that the orders of the royal commission would not be obeyed, and thus made the case against the colony all the darker.

The animus of the board of trade is shown by the fact that they waited neither for the proofs and affidavits of the charges they had sent over nor for the colonies' replies, but on the receipt of a letter from Dudley, dated July 25, 1705, complaining of the slothfulness of the two small colonies in sending men and money for the war,[b] they sent in a representation to the privy council that both Connecticut and Rhode Island continued disobedient.[c] This provoked an order in council of the same date (December 20, 1705), directing them to enumerate the several misfeasances and illegal proceedings of the said charter governments and proprieties in America and the advantages that would arise from reducing them.[d] The board took up the matter with alacrity. By January 10, 1706, it had drawn up an elaborate accusation of the charter governments, repeating, on the authority of Dudley and Cornbury, the charges already cited, and adding to them the general accusations that the colonies broke the acts of trade, did not present their governors for Her Majesty's allowance, denied appeals, made laws contrary to those of England, harbored pirates and deserting soldiers, and the more specific charges that they encouraged woolen manufactures, refused obedience to the royal commissions and proclamations (especially to that in regard to coin[e]), and in general misused the powers intrusted them by their charters and assumed an independency detrimental to the good of the colonies and the Kingdom.[f] Following this general representation, the irregularities of Massachusetts, Rhode Island, and Connecticut were cited in detail, including the report of the Mohegan commission, just received. No mention was made of the Carolinas or Pennsyl-

a B. ef T. Papers, Props., O, 8.

b Ibid., New England, P, 68. Dudley demanded that the quota of Connecticut should be in the same proportion as in the former New England Confederation, 60 to 100 for Massachusetts, which was a disproportionate amount at this time.

c Ibid., New England, Entry F, 65.

d Ibid., New England, P, 67.

e See post.

f B. of T. Papers, Props., Entry E, 238. Printed in part in N. C. Recs., i, 630–633.

vania, but a postscript described the loss of the Bahamas, through the failure of the proprietors to protect them. The result was what the enemies of the charters had hoped—an order in council was speedily drawn[a] to bring in a second bill against the charters, this time in the House of Commons. It was entitled "A Bill for the better Regulation of Charter and Proprietary Governments in America and for the Encouragement of the Trade of this Kingdom and of Her Majesties Plantations," and was a modification of the bill of 1701,[b] omitting New Hampshire and the Jerseys, and making no mention of the "adjacent territories" of Pennsylvania. Instead of repealing certain clauses in the charters, it vested in the Queen the sole power of governing and of appointing magistrates, with a reservation that the laws passed previously by the assemblies and approved by the Crown were to be in force, but hereafter all laws must receive the governor's assent and appeals must be allowed as in her Majesty's other plantations. The bill was submitted for the board's approval,[c] and was presented to the House of Commons by Mr. Blathwayt[d] February 23, 1706.

But the Tory majority was already weakening and Sir Henry Ashurst[e] was able to use his Whig influence to such advantage that the bill never reached a second reading.[f] In fact, the influence of the arch conspirators against the chartered privileges of Rhode Island and Connecticut had begun to wane. Cornbury had made himself so unpopular and had amassed such an array of debts that protests against continuing him in office were already being heard in high places; and spite of his great connections, the Queen was obliged to supersede him in 1708.[g] Dudley, too, found himself in much

---

[a] B. of T. Papers, Props., O, 28, February 7, 1706.

[b] Ibid., Props., Entry E, 324.

[c] Ibid.

[d] House of Commons Journals, xv, 151.

[e] His cousin, Lord Cowper, had superseded a Tory as Chancellor in 1705.

[f] Palfrey, History of New England, iv, 369, says that the bill passed the Commons, but was thrown out in the House of Lords. The House of Commons Journal proves otherwise. Ashurst wrote May 4, 1706: "They brought in a bill last sessions of Parliament to take away your charter, but I made such interest against it with some of the leading men of the House so that it was thrown out at the first reading. I have the vanity to say that if you had not employed me you would have been in a sad condition this day." To the governor and council of Connecticut. Mass. Hist. Colls., 6th series, iii, 384.

[g] S. P. G.—A. MSS. "I hear there is another govr coming for these provinces [New York and Jerseys] people are sorry 'tis another Lord, for they say there never came a good one to these parts."

trouble. He was accused of treacherous correspondence with the French.[a] His friend and patron, William Blathwayt, was removed from the board of trade early in 1707, and, in fact, the entire board was changed and put into Whig hands. Dudley maintained himself by truckling and backing down from all the positions he had taken. In October, 1706, he asked pardon for his zeal and defended himself against the charges of personal interest in the Mohegan matter, protesting against the enmity of Sir Henry Ashurst, and hoping he would not be made a sacrifice to Connecticut and Rhode Island and their agent, who were angry at his obedience to the Queen's commands.[b] In May of this same year Sir Henry Ashurst wrote to Winthrop: "I hope Mr. Dudley for his great guilt will be turned out of his government. * * * I told the Lords that if the Queen would give me £1,000 per annum for me and my heirs to undergoe the trouble and expence I have had (for sixteen years last past) to obstruct the designes and malicious contrivances of one man to oppress and enslave N: England, I would not accept it."[c] But Dudley's power for harming them was nearly at an end. He wrote the new board in most obsequious terms and with great laudations of the Rhode Island authorities;[d] and Ashurst informed the Connecticut authorities that they no longer need fear if they kept within the bounds of their charter privileges and passed no laws repugnant to those of England.[e]

Thus the second attempt to annul the charters of the American colonies by Parliamentary action came to nought. The Whig and dissenting interests in England regained power in time to serve their brethren on the farther side of the Atlantic.

ACT UPON FOREIGN COIN.

The new board of trade, appointed in 1707, adopted a somewhat different method of obtaining information in regard to the proprietary and corporation colonies. Instead of depend-

---

[a] Palfrey, New England, IV, 297.

[b] B. of T. Papers, New England, Entry E, 267. A commission of review in the Mohegan land case was secured by Ashurst, but Cornbury was placed at its head, so Dudley was not censured.

[c] Mass. Hist. Colls., 6th series, III, 324.

[d] B. of T. Papers, New England, Entry F, 463.

[e] Mass. Hist. Colls., 6th series, III, 378.

ing upon the chance information of neighboring royal governors, they sent out a circular letter to all the proprietary
colonies requiring their own governors to give information of
the colonies' condition from time to time, and propounding a
series of questions to be answered as to the number and occu-
pations of the inhabitants, the militia arrangements, the state
of trade and manufactures, and the form of the government. [a]
The answers to these queries form a valuable source of information for the conditions of the colonies in the early eighteenth century.

The policy of the reorganized board in opposition to the
charter privileges does not appear to have taken immediate
shape. But complaints still came to them of illegal trading,
and that the principles propagated in the chartered colonies
infected those under direct royal control and stimulated them
in opposition to the English policy. The specific complaint
that led the board to take action was of their disobedience to
a royal proclamation fixing the values of the foreign coins
that passed current in the colonies. It arose from a report of
the governor of Barbados that the island colonies were being
drained of their coin by those of the mainland, especially
those under proprietors. The lack of a mint in the colonies [b]
and the constant loss of specie by the enforced English trade
made the problem of currency a very serious one. William
Penn wrote in 1701: "The whole continent labours under the
want of money to circulate trade in the respective Governments, which has put Boston herself upon thinking of Tickets
to supply ye want of coyn, and New York as well as this
Province are following." [c] Several of the colonies sought to
maintain a balance of coin in their favor by receiving it at
higher rates than it passed current elsewhere, and a bill passed
by the Massachusetts assembly to that effect attracted the
notice of the board of trade in 1703. The attorney-general
was consulted to know whether the Queen might not by royal
prerogative fix the rates of foreign coin for the colonies, [d] and
he gave it as his opinion that these might be prescribed in the

---

[a] B. of T. Papers, Props., Entry E, 462. A similar form for New York is printed in N. Y.
Col. Docs., V, 5–7.

[b] A proposition to establish a mint was rejected by the board of trade in 1700. Locke,
however, favored the plan. B. of T. Papers, Pl. Genl., D, 43; Journal, E, 110.

[c] B. of T. Papers, Props., G, 12.

[d] Ibid., Pl. Genl., Entry C, 249.

proprieties as well as in other governments. [a] Accordingly
the Queen, after consultation with the lord treasurer, issued
such a proclamation June 18, 1704, [b] and sent it to the proprietors with an estimate made by the master of the English
mint.

The difficulty of enforcing this ordinance was very great.
Governor Evans, of Pennsylvania, wrote that he had published
the proclamation, but that the merchants would not conform
to it. This was due to "no slack in the governor," but to
"that liberty that Trading men will always take in their own
bargains."[c] Cornbury made its nonobservance a cause of
complaint against the Connecticut government.[d] In 1705 the
board consulted the attorney-general, saying that, being daily
pressed by complaints from the plantations of the unsettled
state of coin, they wished to know whether the proclamation
should be revoked or reenforced,[e] to which he replied that the
rates fixed by the proclamation were legal tender throughout
the colonies, but it could not be considered an offense in private persons to receive coins at a higher rate, and that the
mischief could only be remedied, as it had been in England,
by an act of Parliament, laying a penalty on all persons receiving these coins at higher than legal rates. If the governments
of the proprieties made laws to give the coins a higher rate
than that fixed by the proclamation they would forfeit their
charters, or at least the law making powers embodied in
them, but they could not be held responsible for the acts of
particular colonists.[f]

The matter being merged in the bill of 1706, it was not
considered separately until after the failure of that measure.
In 1707 the board took it up again, and on June 10 made a
representation to the Queen in council on the complaint of
the Barbadians, citing the above opinion of the attorney-
general, and requesting a bill for enforcing the proclamation
and also one that propriety and charter governments be
brought under Her Majesty's immediate government.[g] This

[a] B. of T. Papers, Pl. Genl., F, 16.
[b] Ibid., Pl. Genl., G, 1. The estimate of value of foreign coins; pieces of eight varied
from £4 6s. to £3 7½s., according to date and place of coinage.
[c] Ibid., Props., N, 364.
[d] See list of complaints, January 10, 1706, ante.
[e] B. of T. Papers, Pl. Genl., Entry D, 108.
[f] B. of T. Papers, Pl. Genl., H, 20.
[g] Ibid., Pl. Genl., Entry D, 143.

was followed by a similar representation to the House of Lords November 27 of the same year.[a] The Lords' committee ordered the board to lay before them the charges they had prepared against the charter governments of Rhode Island and Connecticut or any propriety government.[b] In response the board sent all the papers connected with the bill of 1706, as well as a copy of the bill itself.[c] The bill for "ascertaining the Rates of Foreign Coins in Her Majesty's Plantations in America" went through Parliament in due course.[d] It provided for fine and imprisonment of any who took foreign coins at a greater than the legal rate; but the rider to forfeit the charters of the colonies was smothered in the committee of the House of Lords and never came before Parliament.[e]

BILL OF 1715.

For several years after this the colonies with charters were exempt from fears of their revocation. Not until 1712 was alarm again felt. The Tory goverment, under the leadership of Bolingbroke, seems to have meditated some sweeping change in the colonial system which should increase the royal prerogative and render the system of government more uniform.[f] This doubtless arose from the negotiations for the peace of Utrecht and the necessity for arranging a government for the new territory ceded by the French. Connecticut appointed a committee to consult with Rhode Island and Massachusetts, and sent their agent £300 to be used in defeating the design.[g] Their precautions were apparently successful, or else the speedy demise of Queen Anne (August 1, 1714) and the break up of the Tory party hindered the fulfillment of the project.

The New England colonies and the dissenting interests throughout America hailed the accession of the first George with great joy. They felt that their difficulties with the

---

[a] Missing in the papers of the board of trade.

[b] B. of T. Papers, Props., P, 16, January 7, 1708.

[c] Ibid., Journal M, 8.

[d] Statutes of the Realm, 6 Anne, c. 30.

[e] This action does not appear to have been known in the colonies or to have created any alarm. Penn was in treaty for a surrender of his government, and his favor at court may have been used to kill this portion of the act.

[f] Connecticut Colonial Records, IV, 410. Their agent, Dummer, informed the colony that a design was on foot for a new modeling of the plantations and an altering in the civil governments. August 1, 1713.

[g] Ibid., 414.

home government would henceforth be slight.   Dudley was superseded by the change.   Quary, their persistent enemy in the customs office, was dead.   Complaints were much fewer than previously and less circumstantial.   Nevertheless, one of the first acts of the new Whig government was to bring in a bill, August, 1715, for the forfeiture of all the charters. The occasion for it was the attack of the confederated Indians upon the South Carolina settlements and the threatened extermination of that colony.   The colonists in despair appealed to the proprietors, and they in turn to the Government, for soldiers and aid in their extremity.   The agents of the colonists, who had recently been sent over to protest with the proprietors against the extraordinary powers granted to Nicholas Trott, chief justice of the colony, had received these instructions: "In case the proprietors do not redress our grievances * * * we direct you to apply yourselves to a superior power."[a]   They lost no time in appealing both to the board of trade and to Parliament,[b] asking that South Carolina might be taken directly under royal government.   The board therefore demanded at once of the proprietors whether, in consideration of military relief furnished, they would be "willing to surrender their Government to the King."[c]   The proprietors promptly refused, saying that several of their number were minors and could not surrender their right, but if the King would advance them money in this exigency he could hold a lien on the colony for repayment.[d]   Thereupon the board laid the matter before the secretary of state, July 19, 1715, and suggested that the King, by legislative action, take the distressed colony directly under his protection.[e]   This seemed all the more desirable since the Bahamas, held by the same proprietors, had lain waste and defenseless for many years.

The committee of the House of Commons, to whom had been referred the petition of the agents and of several merchants on behalf of Carolina, ordered the board to furnish them with all papers they had upon this subject,[f] and August 10 leave was given to bring in a "Bill for the better regula-

a McCrady, History of South Carolina, I, 531.
b House of Commons Journal XVIII, August 2, 1715.
c B. of T. Papers, Props., Entry F, 442.
d Ibid., Props., Q. 48.
e Ibid., Props., Entry F, 454.
f Ibid., Props., Q. 51, 52; Entry F, 461.

tion of Charter and Proprietary Governments."[a]   The following day the board of trade discussed the bill and agreed to
the draft as sent them.[b]   William Popple, their secretary,
was employed in prosecuting it, and August 13 and 15
it passed the first and second readings, respectively.[c]   This
sudden and unexpected danger to the proprietorships and
governments under charters produced a storm of petitions to
save the interest of various persons.   Lord Guilford, guardian
of the minor Lord Baltimore, appealed in his behalf.   The
guardians of the minor proprietors of the Carolinas, as well
as the trustees of the Penn estate and the agents of Massachusetts, Connecticut,[d] and Rhode Island[e] put in their protests.[f]   These petitions and the evident injustice that would
be done to many subjects by the passing of this bill, as well
as the influence of Lord Cartaret (afterwards the famous Lord
Granville, who was already becoming prominent and had
recently become palatine of Carolina), prevailed with the
committee of the House, which smothered the bill in committee.   It was at this time that Jeremiah Dummer wrote his
famous Defence of the New England Charters.   It was not
published, however, until 1721, when it was dedicated to Lord
Cartaret, then secretary of state.[g]

This was the last attempt of the legislative power of England
to vacate all the colonial charters at one blow, and "unsum-
moned, unheard, deprived them in one day" of their valuable
privileges.

DEFENSE OF CHARTERS.

The bill of 1715 had been warded off, but alarm continued
to be felt for the charters.   The Connecticut assembly thought
it necessary to encourage their agent with sufficient money

[a] The text of this bill is not among the papers of the board of trade, nor have I found
it, but evidence points to its being a reproduction of that of 1706.

[b] Ibid., Journals, R., 216, 217.

[c] The desire to increase the Crown revenues was one large motive in introducing this
bill.   Blathwait was now collector of customs revenues for America, and he had reported,
April 14, 1714, that the charter governments did not hold themselves accountable to the
Crown for any report of their revenues.   Cal. Treas. Papers, CLXXIV, 56.

[d] Jeremiah Dummer succeeded Sir Henry Ashurst as agent for both Massachusetts and
Connecticut in 1710.

[e] Richard Partridge was the Rhode Island agent, Palfrey says, appointed for this emergency.   There would scarcely seem to have been time to so commission him.

[f] House of Commons Journal, XVIII, August 10-19, 1715.

[g] Tyler, History of American Literature (New York, 1878), says this was not published
until 1728.   The British Museum copy is dated 1721, and it was the exigencies of that
year that called for its publication,

for extraordinary charges in the future.[a] The new governor
of Massachusetts sought to gain favor with his colony by
promising to defend its charter if attacked.[b] Such precautions
were not needless. Complaints continued to come in from
those who hoped to profit by charter revocation.[c] Cummings,
custom-house officer at Boston, wrote in 1717: "The Charter
Governments are all enemies of the prerogative, and it would
be a service to the Crown if they were all taken away."[d] The
board of trade continued to make to the King representations
to that effect, which might have been more effective had not
that bureau become by this time something of a sinecure and
of slight importance in dictating policy. July 9, 1719, on
presenting some Pennsylvania laws that had been examined,
they reported, "We are of opinion that the plantations will
never be upon a right foot until the dominion of all the proprietary colonies be resumed to the Crown;"[e] and in 1721,
encouraged by their success in placing Carolina under a royal
governor, their representation was sufficiently strong to cause
alarm among the proprietors and the colonial agents.[f] It was
thought wise to publish Dummer's "Defence," and in the
dedication to Lord Carteret he says: "Having lately had the
Honour of presenting the Humble Address of the Province of
the Massachusetts Bay to His Majesty for the continuance of
their Charter Privileges, which they apprehend in some Danger; It seem'd agreeable at the same time to explain the
Right which the Charter Governments have to those Privileges." Then follow his four famous arguments:

" 1. Charter governments have a good and undoubted right
to their charters.

" 2. That they have not forfeited them by misgovernment
or maladministration.

" 3. That if they had, it is not to the interest of the Crown
to accept these forfeitures.

[a] Conn. Col. Recs., IV, 522. Is this a hint of the method by which the bill was defeated?
[b] Mass. Hist. Colls., 5th series, VII, 77. Letter from Governor Burgess, February 13, 1716.
[c] B. of T. Papers, Props., Q, 81. A memorial from a British merchant offering the suggestion that, by taxing the products of Great Britain the colonies " ipso facto forfeit their
charters."
[d] Ibid., New England, V, 134.
[e] B. of T. Papers, Props., Entry G, 204.
[f] This was occasioned by a quarrel between Governor Shute and the assembly in Massachusetts. Palfrey, History of New England, IV, 415, note. The memorial of the board
is printed in N. Y. Col. Docs., V, 603.

" 4. Observations on the extraordinary method of proceeding against charters by a bill in Parliament."

In regard to thé second point at issue, he called attention to the fact that it was impossible for arbitrary power to be exercised in the charter governments, since the people had a remedy in their own hands in the frequent election of magistrates. "The Fact is apparent that these Governments, far from retrenching the Liberty of the Subject, have improv'd it in some important Articles." He instanced the enrollment of lands, the choice of juries, the easy, quick, and cheap redress in the courts of law, as compared with the delays and expense of the English courts. In regard to the third point he wrote:

> The sum of my argument is, That the benefit which *Great-Britain* receives from the Plantations, arises from their Commerce: That Oppression is the most opposite Thing in the Wórld to Commerce, and the most destructive Enemy it can have: That Governours have in all Times, and in all Countries, bin too much inclin'd to oppress: And consequently, it cannot be the Interest of the Nation to increase their Power and lessen the Liberties of the People. I am so sanguine in this Opinion, that I really think it would be for the Service of the Crown and Nation to incorporate those Governments which have no charters, rather than Disfranchize those that have.

And finally, on the method employed during the past twenty years, Dummer concludes:

> It seems therefore a Severity without a Precedent, that a People who have the Misfortune of being a Thousand Leagues distant from their Sovereign, a Misfortune great enough in it self, should UNSUMMON'D, UNHEARD, IN ONE DAY be deprived of all their valuable Privileges, which they and their Fathers have enjoy'd for near a Hundred Years. It's true, the Legislative Power is absolute and unaccountable, and King, Lords and Commons may do what they please; but the Question here is not about *Power*, but *Right: And shall not the Supream Judicature of all the Nation do right?* One may say, that what the Parliament can't do justly, they can't do at all. *In maximis minima est licentia.* The higher the Power is, the greater Caution is to be us'd in the Execution of it, because the Sufferer is helpless and without Resort.

This polemic made a strong impression and had the desired effect. Legislative action against the charters was checked, and the board of trade contented themselves with attempts to secure the voluntary surrender of the charters, either by payment, as in the case of the Carolinas and Pennsylvania, or by making the advantages of surrender apparent to the corporation colonies. The latter plan was tried with Rhode Island and Connecticut during the boundary disputes between those two colonies in 1723. In a representation of the board of trade, to whom the matter had been referred from the privy council, after signifying their opinion in regard to the boundary right, they concluded:

> Considering therefore the matter in Dispute has no relation to private Property, that the contest, which is purely for Government and Jurisdiction has already lasted sixty years * * * it were to be wished they would both voluntarily submit themselves to His Majesty's immediate Government, as some other Colonies have done, and that they might be annexed to New Hampshire. [a]

An order in council was accordingly issued to that effect and sent over for the colonies to consider and reply. [b]

Rhode Island was at this very time petitioning against a bond being taken of her governor to observe the Acts of Trade as contrary to their charter, [c] and this appears to have aided the desire for surrender. The replies of the two colonies were characteristic and interisting. The response for Rhode Island, drawn up by the hand of her aged governor, Samuel Cranston, is rambling, conciliatory, and full of references to her past history and pioneer sufferings. It concludes:

> Upon the whole wee humbly pray that their Lordships will believe wee have a Tincture of the ancient Brittish Blood in our veines and that wee esteem our libertys and property granted by our Royall Charter equall to any Corporation in great Brittain, tho not of like value, and we hope our loyalty and conduct for the service and Interest of the Crown of great Brittaine hath no wayes merritted the forfeiture of so valuable a Blessing. [d]

The answer of the Connecticut authorities is a dignified, courteous protest against a surrender, and a State paper of great ability and force. [e] " We cannot but be sensible," it begins, "of the Justice and Honr. as well as favour of the present Ministry and Administration in the Method which They have thus thought fit to make use of, by referring a Question of such concern as this is, to the Corporations themselves * * *

---

[a] B. of T. Papers, Props., G, 280. March 22, 1723.

[b] Ibid., Props., R, 43.

[c] Ibid., Props., R. 44.

[d] Ibid., Props., R, 46, Newport, November 26, 1723. Not in R. I. Col. Recs., but see iv, 334.

[e] Ibid., Props., R, 49, New Haven, October 28, 1723. The handwriting is that of Hezekiah Wyllys, secretary of the assembly, but doubtless Governor Salstonall superintended the drawing up of so important a document.

whereas other more forcible Methods formerly attempted
have not been thought reconcileable to the Common Rights
holden by the Laws and Customs of our Nation. Of which,
we, of these Corporations, as well as some in Great Britain
have not long since had experience." The paper goes on to
cite the troubles of the reign of James II, and the subsequent
restoration of the charters which was "thought worthy of
that glorious Revolution, which was occasioned by them."
"You are therefore, hereby directed in plainest terms," they
say to the secretary of the board, "to acquaint their Lordships that we can't think It to our interest to resign our
Charter. But on the Contrary, as we are assured, that
we have never by any Act of disobedience to the Crown,
made any forfeiture of the Priviledges we hold by It: So we
shall endeavour to make It manifest, and defend our Right,
whenever it shall be called in question."[a] This firm and
decided refusal seems to have been accepted by the board in
the spirit in which it was tendered, for in 1726, making a
representation on the boundary matter, they reported that
Connecticut and Rhode Island were not willing to be annexed
to any of His Majesty's governments, or to surrender their
charters.[b]

The administrative authorities did not cease, however, to
represent to the Government on every occasion the importance
of a uniform system for the colonies, and the advantage of
seizing all the charters in favor of the King's prerogative.
Thus, in a much-quoted paper on the "State of the Plantations," drawn up in 1721,[c] the board, among considerations
for improving and enlarging His Majesty's dominions in America, recommended that the laws and constitutions of the plantations could be rendered much more perfect if the King's
commands met with due observance in the proprietary and
charter governments.

This is the great obstacle which has hitherto made it impracticable to
put the Plantations in General upon a better Foot, & therefore we shall
beg leave to mention some of those inconveniences, that have arisen from the

---

a These two papers of Connecticut and Rhode Island are printed in full in the Documentary Appendix. It is believed they have not heretofore been published.

b B. of T. Papers, Props., G, 346. Connecticut had another alarm over her charter in
1729 on the question of the intestacy law (see chapter three ante), and instructed her
agents not to go before Parliament, if it would endanger her charter. Conn. Col. Recs.,
VII, 254.

c B. of T. Papers, Pl. Genl., Entry E, 286; also King's MSS. (British Museum), 205. Printed
in N. Y. Col. Docs., V, 591-629.

large powers & Privileges subsisting by virtue of several Charters, granted
by your Majesty's Royal Predecessors, whereby not only the soil but likewise the dominion or Government of several Colonies is absolutely alienated from the Crown, to certain proprietors, who far from imploying the
said Powers and Privileges to the use for which they were designed, as we
find by former reports from this Board, have frequently refused obedience
to such orders as have been given by your Majesty's Royal Predecessors,
have broken thro' the Laws of Trade and Navigation, made Laws of their
own Contrary to those of Great Britain, given shelter to Pirates and Out-
laws, and refuse to contribute to the Defence of the neibouring Colonies
under your Majesty's immediate Government even in cases of the greatest
emergency, altho' they would not have been able to subsist themselves
without the assistance of their Neibours.

The indictment continues, that in general they had shown
"too great an inclination to be independent of their mother
Kingdom" and "that it hath ever been the Wisdom, not only
of Great Britain but likewise of all other states to secure by
all Possible means the intire, absolute and immediate dependency of their Colonies." The most effectual plan would be to
revoke all charters and put the whole of America under one
lord lieutenant or captain-general, from whom all governors
should receive orders and with whom there should be associated two councilors from each plantation.

A novel method was undertaken by the board in this period
of insisting on the acceptance of an explanatory charter, which
defined more closely the privileges granted in the original
document. That for Massachusetts has already been described.[a] In 1730, in a representation to the King on the
question of the Connecticut intestacy law, the board, while
recommending the grant of the petition to confirm the colonial law, suggested that the people of Connecticut also ought
to submit to an " Explanatory Charter," whereby the people
of that colony may be at least as dependent upon the Crown
as were those of Massachusetts. "And we think ourselves
the rather bound in Duty to offer this to His Majesty's consideration because the People of Connecticut have hitherto
affected so intire an Independency of the Crown of Great
Britain that they have not for many years transmitted any of
their Laws for His Majesty's consideration, nor any accounts
of their Publick Transactions."

Nor did the board of trade fail to keep before Parliament
the anomolies of the corporation and proprietary govern-

_____

a See Ch. II, ante.

ments.   In the report made to the House of Commons in 1732[a] attention was called to the fact that Maryland, Connecticut, and Rhode Island were not required to submit their laws for approval or disallowance, and that in the two latter corporations "almost the whole Power of the Crown is delegated to the People," and that it is not surprising that governments constituted like these "should be guilty of many irregularities in point of Trade as well as in other respects."   Also that the trades carried on and the manufactures set up detrimental to the trade of Great Britain were chiefly in New England, where chartered governments with the little dependence which they had upon their mother country and the small restraints they were under rendered this easy.

Again, in 1734,[b] they repeated the same complaints, which led to the resolutions of the committee of the House of Commons already mentioned in regard to the repeal and transmission of laws, and the commissioning of governors in the corporation colonies.[c]   But all these attempts against the charters were without result.   After the purchase of the government of the Carolinas and the Bahamas, only Maryland and Pennsylvania remained in the hands of proprietors.   Of the New England colonies under charters the only one of importance was under a royal governor.   The insignificance of the small corporations of Rhode Island and Connecticut secured their perpetuation.   The ineffectiveness of the representations of the board of trade at this period was in part due also to the obscurity into which it had sunk,[d] and to the determination of the ministers to preserve the status quo and to avoid being plunged in disputes with the colonies.   The functions of the board of trade were almost wholly usurped by the committee of the privy council for plantation affairs, which showed a spasmodic interest only when complaints were made affecting trade and revenue.

The only new proprietary colony organized after the revolution of 1688 was that of Georgia.   Its charter shows the limitations with which the government saw fit to surround even a charitable scheme when asking for a definite patent of incor-

a B. of T. Papers, Pl. Genl., Entry F, 253.

b Additional MSS. (British Museum), 33,028, fo 246.

c See ante, chapter 3.

d The attendance was very small, but two or three being present at the board meetings after 1735.

poration. The trustees were to make a complete report to the secretaries of state and commissioners of trade and plantations each year. The governor must be approved by the Crown and take the usual oath, and the military defense of the province was not to rest with the proprietary governor, but to be in the hands of a royal appointee, the governor of South Carolina. Moreover, conflict between the executive and legislature was to be avoided by withholding the legislative power from the colonists. On the contrary, the trustees were to draw up all laws and ordinances and submit them for approval to the privy council. Finally, the entire government of the colony should revert, after twenty-one years, to the Crown. Clearly the prerogative was to be secured, though the expense and difficulties of founding the colony were to be undertaken by the corporation.

The chief affairs that came before the board of trade in the period between the last bill against the charters and the renewal of the French wars (1715–1744) were of an economic nature, such as the growth of manufactures in the colonies, the issue of paper money, and the import duties on English manufactures. In these matters the colonies under charters stood on a similar footing with the others. The French wars brought again into strong relief the necessity for union, and one of the objections made by Connecticut and Rhode Island to the Albany plan of union in 1754 was the fear that it might conflict with their charter rights. In one dispute, that between the colonists and proprietors of Pennsylvania in regard to taxing the proprietary estates, the board of trade, in opposition to its earlier policy, sided with the proprietors and maintained that the interposition of the Crown was especially necessary to support the prerogative delegated to them.[a]

The decline, therefore, in the importance of the Board of Trade and Plantations, the inertia of the Whig system of government under the two first Georges, and more than all, the vast respect of the English mind for vested interests and the conservatism that maintains the established order of things, had brought it to pass that governments under charter provisions, and thus removed from the direct control of the Crown, endured until the Revolution, and exercised a forma-

[a] Pa. Col. Recs., VIII, 525–552.

tive influence on American political institutions.   The charters proved important only by their negative effect in sheltering the colonies from English interference, but also by furnishing positive ideals of political independence and popular control, which grew more and more powerful as the century progressed.   Well did Quary predict in 1703 that "*a frown from Her Majesty now can do more than perhaps an army hereafter.*"[a]   The frown proving ineffectual in 1703, the army was no more successful three-quarters of a century later.

[a] Harleian MSS. (British Museum) 6273, No. 1.

CONCLUSION.

The following conclusions may be reached, summarizing the results of this study: In the first place, the grants of charters for North American colonies, either to corporations or to proprietaries, ceased when English colonial administration developed and became efficient. Secondly, the period of greatest hostility to the charters extended over about thirty-five years, from 1685 to 1720; and after the overthrow of the Stuart despotism the chief agent in this opposition was the newly established organ of colonial administration, the Board of Trade and Plantations. Thirdly, this period of struggle to vacate the colonial charters corresponds with the time when the board of trade was an active, energetic element in English administration. It seems to reveal a definite purpose on their part to reduce the American governments to a uniform type and to exercise a more complete bureaucratic control over their institutions and development. Possibly this policy was partly due to admiration for French colonial policy. Fourthly, three methods were employed in proceeding against the charters: (1) Dealing with the corporations and proprietors individually, in order to secure the surrender of their governmental powers either voluntarily or by prosecution in the courts; (2) asserting the prerogative within chartered limits and securing some measure of control over the executive, judiciary, or legislature; (3) vacating all the charters at once by Parliamentary action. The last failed entirely, the second succeeded in a limited degree, and the first was the most successful. By its means the charter of Massachusetts Bay was limited; the charters of the Jerseys, the Carolinas, and the Bahamas were yielded up, and that of Pennsylvania was retained in the hands of the proprietors only by accident.

[319]133

In the next place, it may be observed that the loyalty of the colonists to their charters was strongest and the greatest efforts were made to maintain them in the corporation colonies where popular sovereignty found its most complete and consistent expression.   In the proprietaries the attitude of the colonists toward the charters depended entirely upon the measure of protection which the charters assured them, whether in maintaining religious liberty or in developing local democratic institutions.   In other words, only in so far as the proprietors ceased to be the holders of a fief and became the executives of a democracy did the people support their proprietary rights and desire the continuance of their charters.   We must, therefore, question Mr. Doyle's conclusion [a] that it would have been a gain to colonial administration and the development of the American plantations had one of the bills attempted in 1701 or 1706 or 1715 passed into a law.   Had the corporation and proprietary types of colonial government disappeared and all the colonies been assimilated politically to the provincial form, the variety and vitality of American institutions must have been lessened, the ideal of popular sovereignty dimmed, and the growth of democratic forms checked.   In consequence our State and national constitutions would have been less popular, less republican, and less distinctively American than they are.

Finally, the colonies under charters exercised much influence upon the royal colonies and made them restive under administrative control.   As early as 1703 a Pennsylvania judge of the Admiralty wrote that the example of the proprietary and charter colonies put the others "on trying projects and trials of skill with their governors." [b]   About the same time a persistent enemy of charter governments wrote to the board of trade: "This makes the people of the Queen's Governments murmur and repine, and puts them on thinking what should be the reason their next neighbours and fellow-subjects should enjoy more Ease, Liberty and Freedome under the proprietor's Government than they do or can under her Majesty.   And that which aggravates their Discontents, these people of the proprietary Governments make it their business to upbraid and reflect on them as being slaves and miserable

a Doyle, Puritan Colonies in America, II, 402-404.
b Harleian MSS. (British Museum), 6273, fo 1.

in comparison with themselves." [a] The persistence, therefore, of two corporation colonies and two proprietary colonies
until the Revolution has a significance greater than their
importance would denote.   The ideal of colonial government
which they furnished rendered the other colonies dissatisfied,
it paved the way for united opposition to England, and,
after American independence had been won, it played a large
rôle in developing the new governments, Federal as well as
State.

---

[a] B. of T. Papers, Pl. Gen., E 31. The term "proprietary" is used in a general sense
to denote all colonies under charters.

DOCUMENTARY APPENDIX.

NEWPORT *Nov. 26, 1723*

I have communicated Your Letter with the propositions and advice of the Right Honorable the Lords Comissioners for Trade and Plantations etc. to the Generall Assembly of this his Maj[ts] Colony sitting in Newport the 26th of November 1723, who requested mee in their Name to returne the following memorial and answer to their Lordships.

Viz with all due and humble submission they pray their Lordships will be pleased to consider that their Predicessors with great Perrill and charge Transported themselves and Families from their Native Country of Great Brittain to this then a Wild and Howling Wilderness (as great part is to this day) Inhabited by Salvage and Barbarous People, and Beasts of Prey, we shall not Instance or insist on the particulars of the great Sufferings, and cruell hardships they Suffered and encountered with after their arrival in the Massachusetts Bay before they were compelled to seek Shelter and releif among the great Body of Salvage Nations within the precincts & confines of this Colony who (by the Christian deportment and winning behaviour of our Said Predicessors) was by the Divine Providence of God become Gentle and compassionate, considered their distressed condition and granted them Liberty to erect Hutts and digg Cellars among them to Skreen and Shelter them from the Extremity of the Weather and by their Christian demeaniour and conversation as afores[d] the Natives in a Little time became more familiar and sold them considerable Tracts of Land as the Towneship of Providence, Pautuxet, Warwick and Misquament alias Westerly, so that as their number increased they associated together Purchased

---

a B. of T. Papers, Props. R, 46.

Rhode Island and the rest of the Islands in the Narraganset
Bay it will exceed our present purpose to innumerate or par-
ticularize the unaccountable Hardship Labour and discourage-
ment they met with from the Neighbouring Goverments,
and before they could Subdue and Cultivate a little Land to
raise some corne and keep a little Stock of Creatures to subsist them selves and families, but through their great Labour
industry and paines with the Blessing of God they made such
improvement in a few Years, as incouraged them to Petition
his Royall Majesty King Charles the first for a Charter of
Incorporation which they obtained from the Earle of Warwick &ct with Meets, Cutts, and Bounds, the King then being
Imbroiled in the Civill Warrs by his Rebellious Subjects, the
original Charter then Granted, you have with you.

        *   *   *   *   *

We answer to their Lordshipps first proposition about quiet-
ing the difference between this Goverment and the Goverment of Connecticut with humble Submission and due regard
to their Lordships great wisdom we say wee have no difference with the Goverment of Connecticut but what His Majestyes Royall word will determine as afores^d for the obtaining
of which as dutifull and Loyall Subjects shall patiently wait
and doubt not but his Princely Wisdom will influence him to
confirm us in our Just rights and Properties in the possession
of the grant of His Royall Predicessor according to our
Charter.

To the Second proposition insisted upon by their Lordships
viz for the better defence of the Country wee answer that his
Majesty its true may strengthen us with standing Troops but
for any other Strength as we are a Frontier to the Ocian, the
Inlets into our Bay is so open & wide that it is impracticable
to fortifie them so as to prevent an Enemy from entring into
the same tho' at this time wee are Building our Fort more
regular and defencable with Stone and Lime and morter for
the security of Trade and Navigation the Colony having allready given five Thousand pounds toward the carrying on
that work, the Strength of this Colony (under the protection
of God) consists in our Militia who are trained up and exercised in Military discipline and are obliged continually as well
in peace as in warr to be supplyed each man with a good fire
arme powder and ball and they are generally verry expert in

the use of them so that through the Blessing of God wee have
not only defended ourselves against His Majestys & the Colonyes Enemies, but have very frequently offended them both
by Land and by Sea, and upon any expedition against the
King's Enemies have exceeded our quotas with the rest of the
Colonyes and Provinces.

To the third Proposition that Trade may be better secured
&c wee answer as afores[d] that wee are fortifying our Harbour
more Strongly for the Security of Trade &ct. and to enable
our Governour to comply with the Acts of Trade and Nava-
gation, the which he is annually Sworn to observe and the
which he hath to the utmost of his power duly performed in
his circumstance (considering the Constitution of the Govem[t]
obligeth him to be more carefull and circumspect upon that
foot than any that is distinguished by the Name of a Kings
Govern[r] for which many reasons could be given but for brev-
ity's sake shall for bear.

Fourthly to be annexed to New Hampshire besides its being
impracticable, wee answer that our Pridicessors through great
perills labour and hardships as is before recited, left us their
purchases labour and improvements as our Birth right to
which by the favour and clemency of a most gracious King
they Tacked our present Charter full of valuable privileges
&ct and as they with great cost and difficulty obtained and
defended the same against their envious and ungratefull Neighbours and others for the good of their offspring and Posterity,
so we hold ourSelves in duty and conscience bound to endeavour the preservation of so valuable a Blessing, and question
not, but so long as wee continue duitfull Loyall and obea-
dient Subjects to his present Majesty King George and his
Royall Issue but to be protected in our Liberty and property
the which through his Princely goodness he hath so often
declared to maintain and in a most pathetick manner upon his
accession to the Throne.

Fifthly as to our being anexed to the province of New
Hampshire under a Kings Governour wee answer as before
that it is impracticable to be annexed to that Province should
it be our misfortune to have our Charter vacated and taken
from us, the great Province of the Massachusett Intervening
and lying between this Colony and y[t] Province, and with humble Submission wee presume that the Governour of this his

Majesty's Colony is as much a King's Govr as any Governour
in America, by vertue of our Royall Charter under the great
Seal of England and wee esteem him as such during his
administration and he makes the Laws of England his rule
and Gov^{nt} without it be some perticular laws of the Colony
which the Laws of England could not releave us in the not
repugnant and he is under the same restriction and penalty
for any misdemeaniour or Transgression by him committed as
any other of the King's Governours under his Immediate commission and by an Act of Parliament made in the Reigne of
King William the 3d as liable to be called home to great Brittain
to answer the same.

Wee humbly conceive that the vacating and takeing away
Charters of Incorporation granted by the Crowne (without
Just Cause of forfeiture) was never known but in an arbitrary
Reigne as in that of King James the 2^d when all Corporations
and Charters were crush't and Trampled under foot the effects
of which wee severely felt in that short Interval of Sr Edmond
Andrases Goverment whose arbitrary will with a few of his
creatures was a law and the Kings Subjects made Vassals
and Slaves in defiance of Magna charta and the Liberty of a
Brittish Subject wee would not be thought by what is before
recited to make any reflection upon his present Maj'tyes Governours under his immeadiate Commission they being under
the regulation and correction of a most Just and Gracious
Prince who will not suffer or countenance the violating and
infringing the Liberty and property of his faithfull and loyal
Subjects (but as the Proverb is what hath been may be againe)
and our Royall Charter and most Gracious priviledges once
given up there is no prospect of obtaining the same againe.

Wee would have presumed so farr upon their Lordships
favour to have made some remarks upon the difference wee
conceive there is between a Governor under his Majestyes
Immeadiate Commission and a Charter Governor, but that
being allready so truly explained by Mr. Dummer in his Book
put forth in Vindication of Charter Goverments that we
shall not make any further reflections thereon to which Book
wee refer upon that head and sundry others therein sett forth.

Upon the whole wee humbly pray that their Lordships will
believe wee have a Tincture of the ancient Brittish Blood in
our veines and that wee esteem our liberty and property

granted by our Royall Charter equall to any Corporation in great Brittain tho not of like value and we hope our loyalty and conduct for the Service and Interest of the Crown of Great Brittaine hath no wayes merritted the forfeiture of so valuable a Blessing.

*　　*　　*　　*　　*　　*　　*

Signed　　　Sam^{EL} Cranston, *Govern^r.*

REPLY OF CONNECTICUT TO SURRENDER OF CHARTER.^a

N. Haven *Oct 28, 1723.*

Sr. We have rec^d yours of the twentieth of August last, where in you acquaint Us, That, by order of the Rt Honble the Lords of Trade & Plantations, you are directed to enquire of us whether we are willing to resign our Charter to ye Crown? Or, to be more immediately united to the Crown? By ye two Phrases, we suppose the same thing is intended. viz Whether we are willing to part with those Liberties, Powers & Priviledges, which we have so long had & held, by ye Royal Charter granted to this Corporation in the Reign of King Charles the 2nd.

We have also received, a copy of the Order of the Rt Honble the Lords of the Committee of his Majesties most honorable Privy Council, of ye 17th of July last, whereby they have directed, that enquiry to be made; In w^c their Lordships put the Question in other Terms, as intending the same thing Viz Whether we are willing to submit ourselves to his Majesties immediate Government?

We can't but be sensible of the Justice & Hon^r as well as favour of the present Ministry & Administration, in the Method which They have thus thought fit to make use of, by referring a Question of such concern, as this is, to the Corporations themselves. For, If upon any Reasons or Motives that can he laid before us, We should be induced to think it our Interest, to resign to the Crown. w^t Powers we hold, & Priviledges we enjoy by Patent from the Crown, as other Corporations do; and thereupon consenct to be deprived of them, It would certainly prevent all objections or Pretence of

a B. of T. Papers, Props. R. 49.

wrong; which might otherwise be surmiz'd.   And the World
would be obliged to justify such a Method as this, of vacating these Charters, as very fair and impartial.   Whereas
other more forcible Methods formerly attempted have not been
thought reconcileable to the Common Rights, holden by the
Laws & Customs of our Nation.   Of which, we, of these
Corporations, as well as some in Great Britain have not long
since had experience.

Every one knows what a Destruction came on us & Them
in the latter end of the Reign of King Charles ye 2nd. and in
the Reign following.   But that violence was not lasting, what
was extorted from them in form, was soon restored.   And
tho' some of those Corporations were so managed, as to be
induced even to a formal Resignation of their Charters;
Yet, It was the Opinion of the Nation declared in Parliament,
that notwithstanding the Consent so gained, the taking away
& denying to those Corporations, the Powers & Priviledges
enjoyed by their Charters was a Grievance, The relieving of
which, among other things was thought worthy of that glorious Revolution, which was occasioned by them.

But this Method which You are directed to take has not
the least appearance of any Force or Terrour in It.   Nothing
can be fairer than to recommend such a Matter as this, to the
Consideration of the Corporations themselves: That If We
find any Inconvenience in our present State, and think we
could better our selves by a Change, We have Liberty so to
do.   But if we find ourselves in good Circumstances, and
have no prospect of any advantage, if we should resign, &
put an End to our Corporation, by consenting to some other
Form of Government, that then we should be freely at Liberty to continue in our present State; and not come in to the
Resignation recommended to us.

The power of the King & Parliament is as great now as It
was then when another Method was thought proper to be
used with Corporations; And ye Authority of the Ministry
not at all inferior to what It was then: Yet, Its the Glory of
our Times, and a Happiness which no Age or People, ever
had greater Reason to boast of, That, The Powers which a
good Providence has set over us, tho' unlimited or Subject to
none, yet observe the Limits of Wisdom & Justice and are

tender of what others should enjoy, as well as of their own Prerogative.

This gives us great Encouragement & assurance We can remember the time, when the bare mention of such a Liberty, as that which their Lordships have thus led us to the use of, would have been thought criminal. And, We could not have opened our own mouths, to be our own Advocates, Or, presumed to have alledged, That we had not by any means forfeited our Priviledges; Or, Said any thing in defence of them, without danger of incurring the utmost displeasure, both of his Majesty, that then was, & of his Ministry. But, by the great Favour of Heaven the Case is otherwise with us.

We have a king & ministry, who don't make use of their Power to terrify us out of our Rights and Properties, but give us leave to speak for our Selves. And, think It's fit, that what we have, and can't, by force of any Law, be taken from us, should be obtain'd by our own free Consent; (as the only fair way, which even the greatest Prince may make use of) or, otherwise remain in our possession and Enjoyment.

We have therefore thought It our Duty, by Letters, both to the Lords of the Committee of Council & to the Lords of Trade and Plantations, to acknowledge that Regard which their Lordships have been pleased to express for our Charter Rights and Priviledges, in directing that You should inquire of Us whether We are willing to part with them, as what they judged very proper, if not necessary, in order to that change which they seem to recommend to Us.

And, We are not a little concern'd that after such an instance of their Lordships great Regard to our Interest, We should find our selves under a necessity, not to choose that Resignation of our Rights which, They are of Opinion might be best for us. .

But we are perswaded their Lordships will consider the mighty force of enjoyment & experience. All the wisdom of the wisest men in the World, can't relish Priviledges of any kind, as they should that enjoy them. If their Lordships were of the parting side, supposing them in the Possession of any Priviledges, which a long experience had made valuable to them, As we have been of Ours, We dare say, their Lordships would not think It any fault in us, to be loth to part with, or, willing to preserve them. And therefore we presume and hope their Lordships will not impute It to us, tho' we can't come into such a Cession of our Charter as You are directed to propound to Us.

Nor, can we think, If we should do so, we should be more firmly united to the Crown, or more immediately under his Majesties Governm^t, than we are now. Which are the chief considerations you have been directed to suggest on this occasion.

We can't but hope We are as firmly united to the Crown as any of his Majesties Colonies or Plantations. We are under the same Protection; We have not the least Pretence of any Power or Privilege, Estate or Property but what we hold under the Crown. We are subject as any other Colonies to his Majesties Commands and to the Laws provided for them. We are as solemnly engaged in our Fidelity to his Majesty, and have as true & sincere Allegiance to King George as any of his subjects within his dominions.

And we are not only as closely, but as immediately united to the Crown as any other of his Governments. The Bond of this Union (if we rightly understand what is meant by it,) is, on his Majesties part, his Authority or sovereignty over us; and, on our part, our faithful allegiance & subjection to Him.

It seems therefore to us, that His Majesties Authority can't be more immediate in other Governments which have no Charters than it is in this.

The King exercises his authority in them by his Commission, as he does here by our Charters, which is the Kings Commission, to warrant the Authority of the Officers appointed by it here.

The Governours Commission in other Governments, and the Charter in Charter Governments, are both of them immediately from the Crown. So that we conclude, we are as neer to the Crown; and to that Protection from It, which we rely upon, as any other Governments in the King's Dominions can pretend to be; Nor is there any stricter obligation on any of His Majesties Subjects, to a firm allegiance, faithful and constant subjection to his Majesty, and obedience to his Laws, than there is upon us in this Colony; And in Case of Transgression, We [are] as neer, and close to the Crown as any Subjects.

Their Lordships seem also to think, that unless both the Governments, viz Rhode Island & Wee, agree to submit and resign our Charters, there is never like to be any Agreement, about the Bounds between us, or any Peace in these Parts. In this also we have a farther view of their Lordships Favour and great Concern for our Tranquillity. But if all the Circumstances of that controversy were laid before their Lordships, and known to them, as they are to Us We believe Their Lordships would not be of Opinion that the Consent or Resignation proposed would have such effect.

It's true, If our Charters were resigned, there could be no more any such Contention between us, as distinct Bodies Politick, because that capacity would therefore cease. But there might be the same contention, & perhaps greater, among particular Persons, whose particular Rights & Properties, have any Relation to those Bounds. Nor can It be thought that the Peace of the Colonies is so much infringed by this Controversy. The Government of R. Island is in actual Possession, (as they themselves own) of the Land w^c they claim, & we think belongs to us. We don't pretend to disturb them in y^t Possession; It is not wee, but they, that have made the Complaint. If they could have sat still, contented with all they desired, Their Lordships had not been troubled as they now are, with this story.

And if their Lordships would but dismiss their Complaint, They might return home, & live in Peace, without any Molestation.

We indeed should be sufferers, while They would still hold Lands, which this Colony disposed of in Townships 20 years ago & more; But we doubt not this matter will have a good issue one time or other. And even now; If their Lordships would but let them understand, that They must be contented with the Bounds set them in their own Charter, and tell them how those Bounds, must be understood and taken, That would end the Controversey.

They would have no reason to Complain; Nor should we give them the least Trouble in the Law, tho' our Charter be prior to theirs.

We assure you, It is with great uneasyness, that we find ourselves under such a Necessity, That Wee must either relinquish at once all the Priviledges we enjoy by the Royal Charter (which prevail'd with our Ancestors to adventure upon the first settlement of this Colony so chargeable & perillous) Or else, we must decline to comply, with that Resignation of our Charter, which their Lordships have directed you to propose to our Consent.   But this Concern is much alleviated, from the assurance their Lordships have thereby given us, that Our holding these Powers and Priviledges, is not inconsistent with the Law, and on that Account to be denied Us, unless we are willing to part with them; tho' they seem to think It might be most to our peace & interest so to do.   In which we must beg their Lordships to suffer us to enjoy our Desires And if hereafter We shall find any inconvenience in It as to this particular, of holding our Charter still, we must be content to blame ourselves for it.

You are therefore hereby directed in plainest terms, to acquaint their Lordships, that we can't think It to our interest to resign our Charter But, on the Contrary, as we are assured, that we have never by any Act of disobedience to the Crown, made any forfeiture of the Priviledges we hold by It; So We shall endeavour to make It manifest, and defend our Right, whenever It shall be called in question.

What those particular offences, or Acts of Disobedience to the Orders of the Crown, which some Charter Governments have been guilty of: And which you say their Lordships insisted on, as what would prevail with the Parliament to deprive us of our Charters We may not be able to guess.   But, wee dare rely upon the Parliament, that whenever They think fit to inspect the Charters, They will distinguish between the guilty and ye Innocent.

If we have always behaved ourSelves, with a faithful Duty & Allegiance to the King; and have observed the Orders at all times sent us with Readiness; The Parliament will not condemn our Charter & deprive us of all the Benefit of It, because some other Charter Governments have demeaned themselves undutifully; or done w^t is a just forfeiture of their Charter Liberties.

We can't think It will be any manner of Revocation to that August Body of the greatest & best men, that we insist upon

our own Vindication; and can't be willing to loose the Priviledges We enjoy.   When we know we have done nothing to
deserve it.   We are persuaded We have a King on the Throne,
who will esteem It among the Prerogatives of his Crown, to
be the Support & Protector of the Rights of his faithful
subjects.

We are so far from being apprehensive that if the King &
Parliament, should have any complaints made against Us; of
Such a Nature as their Lordships speak of; as, Disobedience
to Orders sent Us; And should think fit thereupon, that the
Matter Should be taken out of the ordinary Course of the
Law; and be tried before them; We say, if the Case should
be so, We can't imagine, that They must needs pass a sentence
of condemnation upon us, When in a legal Process against us
we should be found innocent   Such a Thought as this would
render us worthy of High Displeasure

The King, in that great Court is the Fountain of Equity.
There, we might hope, if we had by any unhappy mistake
deserved a legal Condemnation, to have the severity of the
Law tempered, and not to be stripp'd of all, for an Action,
perhaps inadverdently done, which nevertheless the strict
Justice of the Law might condemn us for.   How much more,
may we be assured, that such a Power as that of the King
Lords and Commons, will ever have a favour for us when
they find we have carefully observed Laws & Orders which
have been given us, & broken none.   As we make no doubt,
we shall be able to shew, whenever there may be Occasion

We might here suggest to you many things in support of
our Charter, and the Rights We hold by It.   And we might
first of all observe The particular Declaration of his Majesty
King Charles the 2ᵈ in our Charter; wherein he takes notice
of the Addition, made to his Dominions, by the settlement
we have made here; which induced him to grant us the Tract
of Land contained in our Bounds; This seems to imply some
thing of the Nature & Right of purchase in It.   And the truth
is, the settlement here made, at our own Cost, and attended
with so much difficulty & danger, may well be look'd on as a
deer purchase.

We may add, to this

That if the Charter be resigned or destroyed, and this Corporation thereupon cease; It will destroy all the Rights &

Properties which the Corporation has & holds (by the Charter only,) as well as the Government. Since It can't, we conclude, be imagined, that there should be a succession in the Corporation, by an annual Election of Officers, to hold the Estate; and at the Same time, another form of civil governments established among us.

That we have never been any particular charge to the Crown in time of Peace or War; but have maintained this part of his Majesties Dominions, as well as gained it at first, at our own cost. While we have only had our part with other of his Majesties Colonies, in the Common Protection, without putting the Crown to the charge of Garrisons or Stores, which are allowed in some Provinces.

That the settling of this Colony, and continuing of It, under a Charter administration has never been any Prejudice to the Crown, but Advantage. As we think we are able to shew in a multitude of instances.

That there is nothing can be justly imputed to us, as a Forfeiture, either in Law or Equity of our Charter, or any of the Priviledges we hold by It.

That what is most commonly objected to the Plantations viz A Familiar Transgression of the Laws of Trade, by managing unlawfull Commerce with Pirats, or with Foreign Nations, or any plans whatsoever, is what we are perfectly free from, and even from any just grounds to be suspected of it.

There are many other things of like Nature, which we could mention; and we dare boldly affirm upon the whole, that we have never done anything willingly, or even ignorantly, which can be look'd upon, in Law or in Equity, a just ground for condemning our Charter. Which we think we hold by the same Right, that our Fellow Subjects do their Lands and Liberties

Yet, Its possible, that those who have suggested so much against Us to their Lordships, as to perswade them to think it our Interest to resign our Charter, may by some means or other, make such misrepresentations of us to the Parliament, as may insinuate It unfit we should be suffered to enjoy It any longer.

If any such thing should happen, We hereby direct you in our Name, to beg that we may be advised of It, and have time allowed us to make answer for ourselves. For as all such accusations must be grounded on some matters of Fact alledged against Us, so It will be impossible, perhaps, by writing from hence, to avoid the force of such misrepresentations. But we must be obliged to send over some Person, who by his long & good acquaintance with our Proceedings, may be able to set such matters of Fact in their true light, and strip them of that obscurity, which they are artfully covered with, that they might be made to look black & criminal.

This is a Duty we owe our selves; who are conscious, that we have never done any thing that can be reasonably thought, a Forfeiture of our Charter. And we doubt not, but by this means, we should sufficiently vindicate Our Selves against all Imputations.

This is all at present, which we need to say, in answer to Your letter. But we must desire you, in acquainting their Lordships that we can't consent to resign our Charter, to assure them, that notwithstanding this, We have a deep sense of their Favour, in the Direction they were pleased to give You to write to us, and refer It to our Consideration.

We ar Sr. Y^r humble Servants.

THE GOV^r & COMPANY OF HIS MAJESTY
COLONY OF CONNECTICUT.

G. SALTONSTALL *Govr*

Signed by order of the Gen'll Assembly,

HEZ. WYLLYS *Sec^r*.

BIBLIOGRAPHICAL NOTES.

I. MANUSCRIPTS.

In the preparation of this monograph seven collections of manuscript material were used, five in London, one in Oxford, and one in Paris.

1. THE PUBLIC RECORD OFFICE PAPERS.

The greater part of the material was found in the British public record office, where the following sets of papers were consulted:

> (*a*) The Colonial Series.
> (*b*) The Treasury Papers.
> (*c*) The patent rolls.
> (*d*) The Admiralty books.

(*a*) The classification and condition of the papers of the Colonial Series have been described by Prof. Charles M. Andrews in the Annual Report of the American Historical Association for 1898, pages 49 to 60. Most of the material utilized in this thesis was taken from the second group of papers—those after 1689, calendared now to 1696—and from the series known as the "Board of Trade Papers."

These papers of the board of trade, comprising 860 volumes in all, are classed as acts—a collection of over 100 volumes of colonial laws submitted for ratification; journals (1691 to 1760); naval office lists; papers concerning the separate colonies, viz: Antigua, Bahamas (after 1717), Barbados, Bermudas, Carolina, North Carolina (after 1730), South Carolina (after 1720), Georgia, Hudsons Bay, Ireland, Jamaica, Leeward Islands, Maryland (1689–1715), Massachusetts (1700–1760), Montserrat, Nevis, New England, Newfoundland, New Hampshire, New Jersey (after 1702), New York, Nova Scotia, St. Christopher's, St. Lucia, and Virginia—and, finally, the two collections known as "Plantations General and the Proprieties."

The latter include both proprietary and charter governments. The classification is inexact. For example, many papers on Connecticut and Rhode Island are found in the Proprieties, and others of equal importance in the New England group. The same is true of New Hampshire and Massachusetts. For the purpose of this thesis the Plantations General, Proprieties, and New England Series were most useful. In each of these series there are two sets of books. The first consists of original documents, letters, petitions, proposals, and the orders in council thereupon. They are bound up together, and the volumes of each series are lettered. The second con tains entries of the more important of the documents in the first series, copies of the replies sent out by the board, and the representations presented to the privy council or to Parliament. These are known as "entry books," and are also lettered. The references are made thus: "Board of Trade Papers, Plantations General A, 16," or "Board of Trade Papers, Plantations General, Entry A, 16."

(*b*) The Treasury Papers are very well calendared, but in a few instances, chiefly those connected with the bills for lob bying, it was necessary to consult the original papers.

(*c*) The patent rolls were consulted for the commissions for the earlier councils of trade and plantations in the reign of Charles II.

(*d*) The Admiralty papers are an important source of material for colonial history. No information regarding the vice-admiralty courts in the colonies is to be found in the records of the high court of Admiralty, but the Admiralty books from the secretary's department contain the journal of that department and the commissions for the officers of the vice-admiralty courts, also materials about the trials of pirates and the condemnation of captured pirates. The series known as the "Admirals' Despatches" deals chiefly with naval matters, but doubtless contains much interesting colonial material. These were not kept and classified until 1745.

2. THE PRIVY COUNCIL REGISTER.

This important series of books is kept at the Government office in Downing street, London. Through the kindness of Mr. Hubert Hall and the chief clerk of the council I was permitted to examine the volumes referring to the period under consideration. After 1696 they were of comparatively little use, since everything connected with the colonies was referred to the board of trade and preserved among its papers. In regard to appeals from the colonial courts, the register gives the decisions of the committee on appeals, which are not to be found in the board of trade papers.

3. THE COLLECTIONS OF THE BRITISH MUSEUM.

Among the Harleian, Egerton, Kings, and Additional Manuscript collections in the museum were found various letters from men of the period, and some documents of importance, notably the "Overtures touching a Councill to bee erected for foreigne Plantations," and the "Instructions" for the council of 1660.

4. THE COLLECTIONS OF THE BODLEIAN LIBRARY.

At Oxford the Clarendon and Rawlinson collections contain letters and private papers of several persons interested in colonial government in the early eighteenth century.

5. COLLECTIONS OF ECCLESIASTICAL DOCUMENTS.

Becoming interested in the relations of the authorities of the established church to colonial administration, I went to Fulham and Lambeth palaces to see what materials had been there preserved. At Fulham the papers are unassorted and unavailable, but I am convinced that those of the eighteenth century have been largely removed and are scattered among private collections. Some of the letters of the Bishop of London I found in the Bodleian at Oxford. At Lambeth, where the manuscripts are preserved and classified, the papers of Archbishops Tennison, Gibson, and Wake were examined. The best material for the study of the colonial church is to be found among the papers of the Society for the Propagation of the Gospel. The records of this society have been most carefully preserved, and by the courtesy of the secretary I was given access to them. They consist of—

First. Letters and reports of missionaries to 1736, twenty-six volumes of carefully copied letters, designated as A MSS.[a]

---

a The abbreviation used in the text is S. P. G.—A. MSS.

Second. Original letters and reports of missionaries in the eighteenth century, classified by colonies, chiefly after 1736, twenty-five volumes in all, known as B MSS.

Third. Journals of the proceedings of the society.

Fourth. Committee reports, forty-seven volumes.

Fifth. Colonial letters to the Bishop of London, 1803–1828.

Sixth. Account books, 1701–1892.

I was able to examine only the earlier documents, to about 1730, but think that much interesting material for later times is to be found in this collection.   When the missionaries were garrulous and communicative, the general conditions of the colonies are reported with vivacity and circumstantial detail.[a]

6. LES ARCHIVES DU DÉPARTEMENT DES AFFAIRES ÉTRANGÈRES.

At Paris the series of memoirs and documents relating to America contain much of interest on the relations of the French and English colonies and the difference in their administrative policies.   The classification is somewhat irregular, and numbers of the papers are not dated.

II. PRINTED COLLECTIONS.

Besides the collections in manuscript, the following printed records and documents have been consulted:

1. English public documents:
> Acts of the Privy Council of England, new series, 1542–1597, ed. by J. R. Dasent. (London, 1890–1903.)
> Calendar of State Papers, Colonial Series, 1574–1696, ed. by W. Noel Sainsbury and J. W. Fortescue. (London, 1860–1903.)
> Calendar of Treasury Papers, ed. by Joseph Redington and William Shaw. (London, 1868–1903.)
> Journals of the House of Commons.
> Journals of the House of Lords.
> Royal Commission on Historical Manuscripts. (London, 1894–1903.)
> Rymer, Fœdera. (3d edition, 1739.)
> Statutes of the Realm. (Records Commission edition.)
> Thurloe, State Papers. (7 vols., London, 1742.)
2. Archives and Records of the Colonies.
> Archives of Maryland (19 vols.), edited by William Hand Browne. (Baltimore, 1880–1889.)
> Calendar of Virginia State Papers (9 vols.), edited by William P. Palmer and H. W. Flournoy. (Richmond, 1875–1890.)

---

[a] A digest of the society's progress has been compiled, 1701–1892. (Third edition, London, 1892.)

Colonial Records of Connecticut (15 vols.), edited by J. Hammond
Trumbull and Charles J. Hoadley, D. D.   (Hartford, 1850–1890.)
Colonial Records of North Carolina (10 vols.), edited by William
L. Saunders.   (Raleigh, 1874–1886.)
Colonial Records of Pennsylvania (16 vols.), edited by order of
the State.   (Philadelphia, 1838–1853.)
Documents relative to the Colonial History of New York (14 vols.),
edited by E. B. O'Callaghan and B. Fernow.   (Albany, 1856–
1883.)
Federal and State Constitutions and Colonial Charters (2 vols.),
edited by Ben: Perley Poore.   (Washington, 1877).
Grants, Concessions, and Original Constitutions of the Province
of New Jersey, edited by Aaron Leaming and Jacob Spicer.
(Philadelphia, 1881.)
Letters from the English Kings and Queens to the Governors of
the Colony of Connecticut from 1635 to 1749, edited by R. R.
Hinman.   (Hartford, 1836.)
New Jersey Archives (19 vols.), edited by W. A. Whitehead.
(Newark and Paterson, 1880–1897.)
Pennsylvania Archives (First Series, 12 vols.), edited by Samuel
Hazard.   (Philadelphia, 1852–1856.)
Provincial Papers of New Hampshire (7 vols.), edited by Nathaniel
Benton.   (Concord and Nashua, 1867–1873.)
Records of Massachusetts Bay, 1628–1686 (5 vols.), edited by
Nathaniel B. Shurtleff.   (Boston, 1854.)
Rhode Island Colonial Records (10 vols.), edited by J. R. Bart-
lett.   (Providence, 1856–1865.)
Statutes at Large of Virginia (13 vols.), edited by William Waller
Hening.   (Richmond, 1809.)
Virginia Magazine of History and Biography (6 vols.).   (Rich-
mond, 1893–1899.)

3. Correspondence and Private Papers.

Andros Tracts (3 vols.), published by Prince Society.   (Boston,
1874.)
Miscellaneous Letters in Massachusetts Historical Society Collec-
tions:
First Series, Volumes V and VI.
Third Series, Volumes VII and VIII.
Fourth Series, Volumes II, V, VIII, and IX.
Penn-Logan Correspondence.   Memoirs of the Historical Society
of Pennsylvania.   Volumes IX and X.   (Philadelphia, 1870.)
Randolph, Edward: Toppan, ed. (5 vols.), published by Prince
Society.   (Boston, 1898.)
Sewall, Samuel, Diary of: Massachusetts Historical Society Col-
lections, Fifth Series, Volume VII.   (Boston, 1882.)
Talcott Papers, edited by Mary Kingsbury Talcott.   Connecticut
Historical Society Collections, Volume IV.   (Hartford, 1892.)
Winthrop Papers: Massachusetts Historical Society Collections,
Sixth Series, Volumes III and V.   (Boston, 1889.)

4. Pamphlets.

Abstract of Charter for the Society for the Propagation of the Gospel. (1702.)

Account of the Society for the Propagation of the Gospel. (1706.)

Dummer, Jeremiah: A Defence of the New England Charters. (London, 1721.)

Mather, Cotton: Parentator. (1724.)

Pollexfen: Discourse of Trade, Coyn, and Paper Credit. (London, 1697.)

Some Considerations on the French settling on the Mississippi. (London, 1720.)

Thomas, F. S.: Notes of Materials for the History of Public Documents. (Private publication, London, 1846.)

(The above pamphlets are all in the British Museum.)

II. SECONDARY WORKS.

The larger portion of this study being drawn from manuscript sources, the references to secondary works are comparatively few and by no means constitute a bibliography of the subject. The following are those to which reference has been made in the notes:

1. General histories and biographies:

Cobbett: Parliamentary History of England. (London, 1806–20.)

Fitzmaurice: Life of Shelburne. (London, 1892.)

Frothingham: Rise of the Republic of the United States. (Boston, 1872.)

Hakluyt: Collection of Early Voyages. (London, 1812.)

Janney: Life of William Penn. (Philadelphia, 1883.)

Lecky: History of England in the Eighteenth Century. (New York, 1878–1890.)

Pike: Constitutional History of the House of Lords. (London, 1894.)

Stubbs: Constitutional History of England. (Oxford, 1874–1878.)

Tyler: History of American Literature. (New York, 1878.)

Walpole, Horace: Memoirs. (London, second edition, 1847.)

2. Local histories:

Adams: Three Episodes of Massachusetts' History. (Boston, 1892.)

Alden: New Governments West of the Alleghanies before 1780. University of Wisconsin Bulletin. (Madison, 1897.)

Brown: First Republic in America. (Boston, 1898.)

Doyle: Puritan Colonies in America. (New York, 1882–1887.)

Hutchinson: History of Massachusetts Bay. (London, 1760.)

Lucas: Historical Geography of British Colonies. (Oxford, 1890.)

McCrady: History of South Carolina under the Proprietary Government. (New York, 1897.)

Palfrey: History of New England. (Boston, 1858–1890.)

Poyer: History of Barbados. (London, 1808.)

Shepherd: History of Proprietary Government in Pennsylvania. Columbia University Studies, Vol. VI. (New York, 1896.)

Smith: History of New Jersey. (Trenton, 1890.)

Sullivan: History of District of Maine. (1795.)

Trumbull: History of Connecticut. (New Haven, 1818.)

Winsor (ed.): Memorial History of Boston. (Boston, 1880–81.)

3. Administrative Histories:

Benedict: Admiralty Practice in the United States. (N. Y. and Albany, 1894. 3d ed.)

Bonnassieux: Les Grandes Compagnies de Commerce. (Paris, 1892.)

Cawston and Keane: Early Chartered Companies. (London, 1896.)

Clark: Summary of Colonial Law. (London, 1834.)

Egerton: Short History of British Colonial Policy. (London, 1896.)

Hall: History of Customs Revenue in England. (London, 1892.)

Hobbes: Leviathan. (London, edition of 1839.)

Jameson: "Old Federal Court of Appeal," American Historical Association Papers, Vol. III. (New York, 1889.)

Lord: Industrial Experiments in the British Colonies of North America. Johns Hopkins University Studies. (Baltimore, 1898.)

Osgood: "Corporation as a type of colonial government," Political Science Quarterly, 1896.

Osgood: "Proprietary as a form of colonial government," American Historical Review, 1897.

Pownall: Administration of the Colonies. (London, fourth edition, 1768.)

Reinsch: Colonial Government. (New York, 1902.)

Reinsch: English Common Law in the Early American Colonies. University of Wisconsin Bulletin. (1899.)

Tanner: "Colonial agents," Political Science Quarterly. (1901.)

Turner: "Western State making in the Revolutionary era," American Historical Review. (1895.)

Wallis: "Early colonial constitutions," Royal Historical Society Transactions. (1896.)